Tradition, Archaeological Heritage Protection and Communities in the Limpopo Province of South Africa

Innocent Pikirayi

T0396779

Organisation for Social Science Research
in Eastern and Southern Africa (OSSREA)

ISBN: 978-99944-55-68-3

Copyediting: *Matebu Tadesse and Abiye Daniel*
Design/Formatting: *Alemtsehay Zewde*

Organisation for Social Science Research
in Eastern and Southern Africa (OSSREA)
P.O. Box 31971
Addis Ababa, Ethiopia
E-mail: ossrea@ethionet.et
Web site: http//www.ossrea.net

OSSREA acknowledges the support of Swedish International Development Co-operation Agency (Sida), Norwegian Agency for Development Co-operation (NORAD), Netherlands Ministry of European Affairs and International Cooperation, International Development Research Centre (IDRC), and Danish Development Agency (DANIDA).

To my son, Tafadzwa Innocent

Table of Contents

Preface

When this project was initially conceived, my objective was simply to present a perspective of how local and indigenous communities in the northern part of South Africa preserved and conserved archaeological sites or sites connected with the 'more recent past', that is those sites remembered in recent, mostly oral, histories and critical to communities' historical origins and cultural identities. As such, the project was conceptualized within the framework of cultural heritage conservation. Some of this work has been conducted in eastern and western Africa (Joffroy 2005) but none in southern Africa; and thus, in my view, there was a knowledge gap on the subject of cultural heritage conservation in the region. As it turned out, this was proved incorrect in that numerous unpublished technical reports on this subject do exist in southern Africa, mainly in Botswana, South Africa and Zimbabwe.

The thrust of this research project was altered markedly by circumstances encountered in the field. This should be expected of any research because if the results were to confirm what was anticipated during the formulation stages of the research design, the research efforts would not have been justified. Archaeological site condition surveys, and occasional site visits, as it turned out, only provided limited information regarding conservation in terms of what methods of intervention were required to stabilize some of the sites encountered in the study. It was my encounter with local communities that broadened the scope of this work, and transformed it into a project in public archaeology: how the communities and the public accessed, interacted and used some of the sites, and/or negotiated with the past *in the present*. Public archaeology is the study of the relations between archaeology, archaeologists and society in every aspect of daily life. According to Jaime Almansa Sanchez, editor of *Public Archaeology; AP: Online Journal in Public Archaeology*, while acknowledging the problems encountered in defining what it is, he saw it as archaeology in the present tense, with the different issues that affect it and its relations with the public.

Throughout this work, I use the term 'cultural heritage'. Over the last two decades, heritage has become an increasingly important concept in a variety of different traditional and interdisciplinary fields. It is an emergent focus of research for scholars and practitioners in fields ranging from tourism and environmental studies to archaeology, anthropology, art, architecture, and history. Heritage has complex layered historical, symbolic, economic, political, social and religious meanings and applications, and has value to specific groups of people and communities. In this work, I also adopt the OSEA approach to heritage where the term is best understood as a way of interacting with the world in the context of the present. However bloated this perception maybe, a broader objective is to develop practical ways of studying and engaging heritage issues through a new theoretical framework (www.osea-cite.org/what_is_heritage.php).

Recently, Watkins and Beaver (2008) have devoted an article debating and discussing its meaning and scope and its role among communities. According to Shephered (2008), the term heritage provides a paradoxical conceptual space, but this paradox is key to understanding its social effects. The notion of heritage offers a language through which to discuss contested issues of culture and identity, among others, in a postcolonial context, and hovers between individual and collective conceptions of history and sits uneasily between past and present. To quote, "Heritage is *of* the past *in* the present, but the exact nature of this relationship seems unclear" (Shephered 2008, 117). It is within the same context that I use the term 'tradition' in this work. According to Boonzaier and Spiegel (2008, 195), many are of the opinion that tradition is something that asserts that if people are to maintain their socio-cultural identities, they must accept certain behaviour patterns that are required of them. In my view, the term does not imply a 'return' to the past. Rather, I accept the argument by these authors that appeals to tradition are in effect people's efforts to adapt to the contestations and competitive demands of the world.

This project was also formulated within the framework of culture and indigenous knowledge systems. This refers to an alternative and very broad range of informal forms of knowledge as spelt out by Horsthemke and Green (2008), covering local, traditional, aboriginal or Oriental or African beliefs, practices, customs and worldviews. These authors interrogate the term very heavily arguing that there is no single universal knowledge, but rather, all knowledge is produced with relevance to specific contexts and questions. They further point out that knowledge must be evaluated within these contexts, engaged carefully with practices of producing and justifying it across all fields, in order to offer a more conducive environment to a wide range of practices. However, adopting the framework of traditional knowledge systems meant amassing information from the communities in the research area on some teachings and experiences passed on from generation to generation, and, concerned with cultural heritage preservation and conservation. It required crafting knowledge on how such places evoke a sense of country and place, the communities' total environment and world view. This is a specialist study in landscape local histories, and given the complexities of Venda histories and ethnicities, the scope was considered too open-ended to be satisfactorily addressed by the project. Evidently, knowledge gaps exist in the field of indigenous knowledge systems for many southern African societies, and current discussion on this subject seeks to preserve and protect such systems as a means of attaining sustainable development, at least at the policy and development programme levels. While academics still show considerable interest in this field of study, there is lack of focus and resolve in terms of the role indigenous knowledge plays in society, and how such knowledge should be treated in relation to other forms of knowledge. However, the term 'indigenous' is problematic in a southern

African context, as it has been heavily contested, politicized and racialised to such an extent that it proved to be of little relevance to this project (see Watkins 2005).

In this work, I view cultural heritage conservation in traditional contexts as a cumulative set of practices and procedures maintained and developed by peoples with long-term histories of interaction with their natural environment. Like traditional knowledge systems, traditional conservation is part of a cultural complex that encompasses societal and worldview. Conservation approaches must derive from traditional knowledge and resource use (Redford and Padoch 1992; Redford and Mansour 1998). The use of such knowledge in conservation (Cunningham 1996 and 2001) allows for effective management and partnerships to ensure the success of such efforts. Current conservation approaches must address contemporary human needs and practices (Bennett 1992). If conducted in isolation, they become irrelevant and disoriented.

Ultimately, this project is about the relevance of archaeology as an avenue of acquiring aspects of local community knowledge systems, its image among local communities, its political impact and economic potential, its presentation to those communities and the public, etc. According to Cunliffe, Gosden, and Joyce (2009, xiii) archaeology is no longer a luxury, as all cultures in the world are concerned with their pasts and developing various ways to create or reclaim their histories. Archaeology has European colonial origins, but since then, has become a vital technological tool for many people in the world who are attempting to locate their own past or understand the past of others. It has become "a means whereby people from many cultural backgrounds can participate in and discuss issues of mutual interest, local or global". In this vein, it has become an arena for debate and discussion, making it necessary to ask what archaeology was, is, and will be for the vast array of people participating in it. According to Cunliffe, Gosden, and Joyce (2009), the range of activities, modes of thought, and patterns of engagement connected with archaeology are so large as to bring into question whether it is a single subject at all. In this work, I prefer to conceptualize archaeology in the plural— archaeologies— to address this complexity and challenge, but at the same time perceive the view of these authors that it is both a global discipline and a series of local practices. In this vein, it is still plural, if not diverse.

Any history of archaeology will demonstrate how in the past communities and the general public became increasingly ostracized from the subject, and from the sites or heritage in which archaeology focused. This in itself is a disengagement process, which was an integral part of the colonial and other agendas, which created a rupture between western forms of scholarship and non-western traditions. Many scholars have commented on this. It is this non-western tradition here, which constitutes communities and the public, who feel or felt that "archeology has ignored, undervalued or appropriated elements of their past" (Cunliffe, Gosden, and Joyce 2009, xv) and cultural regeneration can only be achieved by claims on the archaeological heritage and the landscape around it. One of the projects reported here relates to the repatriation of human remains excavated by archaeologists on the site of Mapungubwe Hill, Bambandyanalo as well as the surrounding cultural landscape in the middle Limpopo Valley. In my view, it was an issue in-self reflexivity by archaeologists and cultural heritage mangers concerned in the process, in realizing the benefits of preventing perpetuating harm and violence towards communities that archaeology may have caused in the past. The relevance of archaeology in this instance may be realized through dialogue with claimant communities, as well as accepting that conduct of certain archaeological projects in the past may have carried acute ethical implications. I also add that the reburial exercise was to some degree a practice in cultural heritage conservation which carried far more weight to local communities, compared to the restorative works on stabilization. (Nienaber and Hutten 2006).

One study alone cannot form the basis for action. We need diverse and complementary studies to produce solid policy guidelines and other recommendations for effective engagement between archaeologists, heritage practitioners, the community and the public. This study should at least be evaluated as an academic critique on matters of community engagement in particular and public archaeology in general. At most, it is an application of both of these in a particular context, and in a specific region of the world where such archaeologies are in the nascent stages of formulation. These archaeologies are informed by experiences elsewhere— at least conceptually— but specifically confronting the dominant issues and challenges around self-reflexivity, sharing of knowledge about the past, and decolonization in a post-apartheid environment. After all this has been said and accomplished, a critical question remains: Is southern Africa moving towards community-based archaeology or is archaeology still at a stage where one regards it as simply 'reactive' or 'consent-based' community involvement. Although the advantages of moving in this direction are immense in terms of addressing and reshaping the structure of communication with descendant and other communities, indications are that we may not have attained a truly community-based archaeology.

Acknowledgements

I am grateful to the Organization for Social Science Research in Eastern and Southern Africa (OSSREA) for sponsoring this project through a grant for senior scholars. South African National Park (SANParks) permitted this research. My family remained a source of support and patience, as they endured my many trips away from home, in the field and abroad. Some of the conclusions here emanated from numerous discussions with friends and colleagues in the field of archaeology and heritage management. Particular mention goes to Munyaradzi Manyanga, Shadreck Chirikure, Edgar Neluvhalani and Tshimangadzo Nemaheni. Muhadi Vele conducted the interviews in much of Venda, at Dzata, in Thohonyandou, and in Makhado. I thank him for being able to talk to the various age groups on matters of cultural heritage. Tracy Thingahangwi Tshivhase assisted with some Venda spellings. Finally, I owe considerable gratitude to communities from Venda, whose voices and emotions I tried to capture in this study during the repatriation and reburial of their ancestors to and at Mapungubwe. Without them, archaeologists and cultural heritage professionals have no basis to claim authority on the study and management of heritage and knowledge of the past. However, the accountability for the interpretations contained in this work and errors that may be there remains my own.

Abstract

This study captures community voices in matters relating to their relationship with specific archaeological heritage sites and landscapes in the Limpopo Province of South Africa. Focusing on the stonewalled archaeological heritage associated with Venda speakers, and the reburial of human remains excavated by the University of Pretoria from the Mapungubwe and nearby sites. It tries to establish why archaeology and cultural heritage conservation struggles for relevance in contemporary South Africa. In articulating the relevance of archaeology in South Africa in particular and southern Africa in general, and in the context of public or community-based archaeology, this study seeks answers to how communities and the public interact, use and/or negotiate with their pasts. The research critiques the notion of archaeological heritage conservation and attempts to explore the conservation perspectives of descendant communities. It indicates that such perspectives are not in tandem with what archaeologists and heritage managers prescribe. By following the re-burial of human remains from Mapungubwe, the study indicates that descendant communities and individuals can locate their own pasts in cultural heritage sites and landscapes in ways markedly different from modern forms of environmental and cultural resources conservation. This may have nothing to do with academic archaeology. The research further exposed the conflict between cultural heritage protection efforts and modern development and questions the role of such efforts, given the challenges of unemployment, social inequality and poverty. Researchers are therefore encouraged in this study to continue rethinking the notion of heritage, to debate the objectives behind cultural heritage conservation and explore the relevance of archaeology today. It is necessary to share the findings of scientific archaeology with communities and the public for a better understanding of the past.

Key words: Archaeology, relevance, tradition, public, community, cultural heritage conservation, engagement, sharing the past

CHAPTER ONE

Archaeological Sites, Archaeologists and Communities in the Middle Limpopo Basin, South Africa

1.1 Background to the Research

In 2003, the archaeological site of Mapungubwe in the middle Limpopo Valley of South Africa was placed on the prestigious UNESCO World Heritage List. The associated landscape contains evidence for an important interchange of human values that resulted in significant cultural and social changes in the southern African region between AD 900 and 1300. The landscape has archaeological evidence attesting to the existence of a state society, which at the time, seems to have been the largest in the region. This state had trading connections with eastern Africa and Asia, attesting to the exchange of human values. Scientists have also documented evidence of climate change in the area, which archaeologists have used to model the growth and demise of the kingdom based on and around Mapungubwe hill. The kingdom is thus testimony to a culture that became vulnerable to irreversible change. Mapungubwe is only one such site in a much broader cultural landscape spread across northern South Africa, eastern Botswana and southern Zimbabwe in what is now referred to as the Shashe-Limpopo basin. The archaeological heritage found in this region—dominated by both stonewalled sites and non-stone walled settlements— is important in southern African history, as it is a living record of ancestral Karanga, Venda, Tsonga, Sotho and Tswana prehistoric capitals and agro-pastoral villages and towns. Some of these settlements are receiving protection in line with national and international cultural heritage management standards. Skeletal remains exhumed by archaeologists from the sites of Schroda, Bambandyanalo, Mapungubwe, Hamilton and others were recently re-buried in the area with the assistance of local communities and government, setting a precedent in South African archaeological heritage management around the issue of restitution and repatriation.

Communities in the research area have, since the late 19th century, encountered archaeology and archaeologists. However, the practice of archaeology then and until recently, was essentially 'colonial', hence the contestations which followed as a result of dispossession of sites and places considered sacred or ancestral by some descendant communities. European communities became the new local or residential communities as they acquired land for farming, mining, hunting and other purposes. The appropriation of land meant some of the values which are now being upheld as central to the conservation of these sites were completely misplaced or isolated.

The purpose of this research is to establish mechanisms for sharing knowledge, methods and approaches between professional archaeologists and local communities in parts of the Limpopo Province of South Africa (Map 1). By examining selected archaeological sites in the region and evaluating the manner in which archaeologists are conserving and preserving them, and by interviewing some communities on how best to look after these places, the research attempts to explore ways in which archaeology as a discipline can be made relevant and usable by descendant communities.

Map 1: Map of the Limpopo Province of South Africa

SOURCE: Adapted from http://www.places.co.za/maps/limpopo_map.html

1.2 Statement of the Problem

It has been realized that archaeologists working in the world of cultural resources management are as much managers of archaeological material remains that are found within land-use mediators of differing conceptions and values of the past, including what may be regarded 'meaningful' heritage (see Reser and Bentrupperbäumer 2005). For most who strive to make a living from such archaeology, this role is once more manufactured by the logistics of being situated, ultimately by the State, at the intersection of contested values and universal rights (state, landowner, users, indigenous groups, publics), than it does from an internal, reflexive consideration of contemporary archaeological practice in the service of legislated conservation regimes. According to Reser and Bentrupperbäumer (2005) some reflexive considerations need to be applied to this accidental role and consider the ongoing implications for archaeology more broadly when the vast majority of practitioners worldwide operate daily in this contemporary theatre of 'managing' the past.

As archaeology became a scientific discipline, it participated in social debates by providing evidence of past human behaviour. This role was validated in countries with legislation to regulate its practice and protect the archaeological record. Archaeologists developed tools to respond to this expectation, leading to cultural resource management. Driven by concern for data collection for impact and significance assessments, and, given the constraints of time and resources, the role of archaeology is often limited to fulfilling legal requirements. But, archaeology is essentially an academic discipline, where research questions are guided by social and scientific issues. To the public, this presents a view whereby archaeology is a painstakingly slow and labour-intensive discipline which only benefits its practitioners and those who find its discoveries fascinating. Furthermore, the public do not even distinguish in layman terms between archaeology, palaeontology, physical and social or cultural anthropology. In situations where archaeology is conducted in the service of development, its findings are often contested by either developers who are eager to proceed with their projects or by those communities whose heritage is being impacted on. This research views this kind of approach to archaeology as one-sided and therefore not beneficial to society.

In Africa, archaeology has always been conducted on sites by 'foreigners' as archaeologists have worked on sites related to indigenous or local communities. Thus the methodologies used to investigate these places are 'foreign', meaning that they apply conventional Western scientific approaches, with no relevance to local communities in Africa, particularly in matters of site interpretation, presentation and conservation. These colonial roots of archaeology negated indigenous communities and rarely used local knowledge to interpret the evidence recovered. Very often archaeological sites are given arbitrary names due to lack of knowledge about their pasts, and particularly the local or indigenous communities historically linked to or associated with them. Recent approaches to manage some archaeological sites with the assistance of local communities have revealed that these play a critical role in heritage conservation (Ndoro 2001). In parts of the world, including Australia, Asia and the Americas, this 'community archaeology' (Marshall 2002) is now seen as defining the future direction of the discipline. While this research partly advocates this approach, it primarily seeks to redefine the value and relevance of archaeology in southern Africa by upholding community interpretation of cultural heritage, community inclusion in site management, and an understanding of cultural heritage situated within the community (see Chirikure and Pwiti 2008; Chirikure *et al.* 2010).

Following the end of apartheid rule in South Africa, the country was faced with the problem of conserving archaeological heritage in line with international best practices. This witnessed the ascendancy of cultural heritage management in the conservation of archaeological sites and associated cultural landscapes. Heritage managers also placed a moratorium on the excavation of prominent archaeological sites of either national or world heritage status, a move that was perceived as welcome by local, descendant communities, as this ensured the preservation of some of the cultural values for which the significance of these sites was placed. However, the management of some of these sites by national heritage or provincial heritage agencies, who, on the recommendation of archaeologists, nominated them for World Heritage listing, created a dilemma for heritage managers as this distanced local communities from them. This pitted heritage managers, stakeholders (local, non-descent communities) and the state on the one hand, and descent communities and the general public on the other. Further to this was the treatment of archaeological sites as heritage resources worth exploitation, a development that has not been well received by descent communities. In the same vein, when some of the values ascribed to such sites by archaeologists are not in tandem with those of local descent communities, archaeology embraces an ambivalent role. Ultimately, the relevance of archaeology in a post-colonial context lies in repositioning current research approaches to address specific local problems. This research argues that incorporating local knowledge is key in making archaeology relevant in the present.

1.3 Research Questions

In trying to articulate the relevance of archaeology in modern day South Africa and southern Africa in general, and in the context of public or community-based archaeology, this project sought to answer three research questions.

First, how do communities and the public in the research area access, interact and use some of the sites and negotiate with the past *in the present*? A corollary to this question lies in identifying barriers to access, interaction, use and negotiation with the past.

Secondly, when communities make references to preservation of archaeological heritage, what exactly do they mean? Is this meaning in tandem with what archaeologists and heritage managers prescribe? Alternatively, how do people locate their own pasts in cultural heritage places such as archaeological sites?

The third research question arises from recent developments in the research area connected with repatriation and restitution and the granting of a license to a mining company to exploit an area adjacent to a world heritage cultural landscape. Given the reactions of archaeologists, environmentalists, stakeholders and other interested persons, the main question lies in defining current and future directions in southern Africa's archaeology. Is public archaeology or community attainable in South Africa following current developments? Can archaeology be truly in the service of humanity, presented with the challenges of unemployment, poverty, and community development?

These questions are discussed in detail in this study and tentative suggestions are given.

1.4 Research Objectives

When this project was initially conceived, it sought to document existing methods of cultural, specifically archaeological, heritage conservation and, in the process, recommend ways to protect such heritage and raise the conservation awareness among communities living in the Limpopo Province of South Africa. The second objective of the project was to document local community attitudes regarding the recent re-burial of archaeological remains from the Mapungubwe Cultural Landscape, particularly the relevance of the process to traditional methods of cultural heritage conservation. Realising that Western conservation approaches have a limited capacity in protecting African cultural heritage, if not used in conjunction with approaches specific to African local contexts, the research seeks to engage local communities in order to collect 'local' or 'traditional' data relevant for the protection and conservation of archaeological sites or cultural landscapes. These objectives were reshaped as I was presented with an opportunity to explore, through community engagement, the possibility of a project in public archaeology—the study of the relations between archaeology, archaeologists and society in every aspect of daily life.

The first objective sought to understand how the communities and the public accessed, interacted and used some of the sites, and/or negotiated with the past in the context of today. The second objective of the project was understanding the meaning of the term cultural heritage as applied to the local contexts, and how this related with global discussions on the subject, and how communities interacted with the world in the context of the present. The third objective was to attempt to discover how cultural heritage professionals and local, especially descendant, communities, communicated matters of cultural heritage. I use the term sharing in an interactive sense to gauge the level of understanding and dialogue between the two; or the conflict between tradition (traditional knowledge included) and perceived science or best professional practice.

As originally conceived, the primary objective of this work would have been to develop a framework that sought to integrate Western and traditional or local conservation approaches in the protection of southern Africa's archaeological heritage. In doing so, the research would have proceeded to develop appropriate conservation methods that complement Western conservation sciences and traditional indigenous knowledge in cultural heritage conservation. However, the new objective of the research project became that of the relevance of archaeology for acquiring local community knowledge system, its image among local communities, its political impact and other potential, its presentation to those communities and the public. This objective is in tandem with the goals of public archaeology.

1.5 Archaeological Characterization of the Research Area

Although the most well known archaeological sites are located on the confluence of the Shashe and Limpopo rivers, and these are Mapungubwe and Bambandyanalo (K2), the Limpopo Province north of the Soutpansberg is rich in archaeological sites and monuments attesting to settlement since Late Stone Age or Iron Age times. The stonewalled cultural heritage is connected with the Mapungubwe and post-Mapungubwe state (Huffman 2005 and 2007) and sites linked in tradition with Venda history (Huffman and Hanisch 1987; Hanisch 2008) (Map 2). More archaeological surveys have demonstrated the richness of this heritage in adjacent countries (Manyanga 2007; Mothulatshipi 2009), showing settlement continuity from the decline of Mapungubwe state in the late 13th century to the 19th century. Despite this wealth of archaeological knowledge, the settlement dynamics of the Limpopo Province in general, and the middle Limpopo valley in particular, are still poorly known.

The middle Limpopo valley may be considered as a southern extension of what Huffman (1996) refers to as the Zimbabwe Culture area. Numerous stonewalled sites found in this area as well as in adjacent Venda to the south define a cultural landscape that is rich in history and tradition, with some of the sites considered sacred among descendant populations (Hanisch 2008). Some of these sites are closely attached to descendant communities, mostly Venda speakers, for example, Mapungubwe, Thulamela, Makahane, Dzata, Tshaulu, Zwaluvhimbi (Hamakuya), Luvhimbi (Haluvhimbi), Tshilavulu (Thengwe) and Tshitaka tsha Makoleni (Mianzwi), to mention a few (Nemaheni Tshimangadzo, pers.com). Some of these are now part of different historical archaeological and cultural heritage programmes as communities seek to claim their pasts and land which was appropriated through European land alienation and policies arising from racial segregation. This has resulted in increased documentation of the archaeological heritage since many of these sites, some of them mentioned in both written and oral accounts, have not been fully identified and researched. Heritage professionals are of the view that known sites are now facing a wide range of conservation and preservation challenges, including neglect and vandalism. On the contrary, local communities view the apparently ruinous state of such sites as marking the presence of their ancestors, and as such requiring no intervention. However, there are compelling cases for conservation since, as demonstrated in the foregoing presentation, the actions of archaeologists have destroyed some of these sites quite considerably.

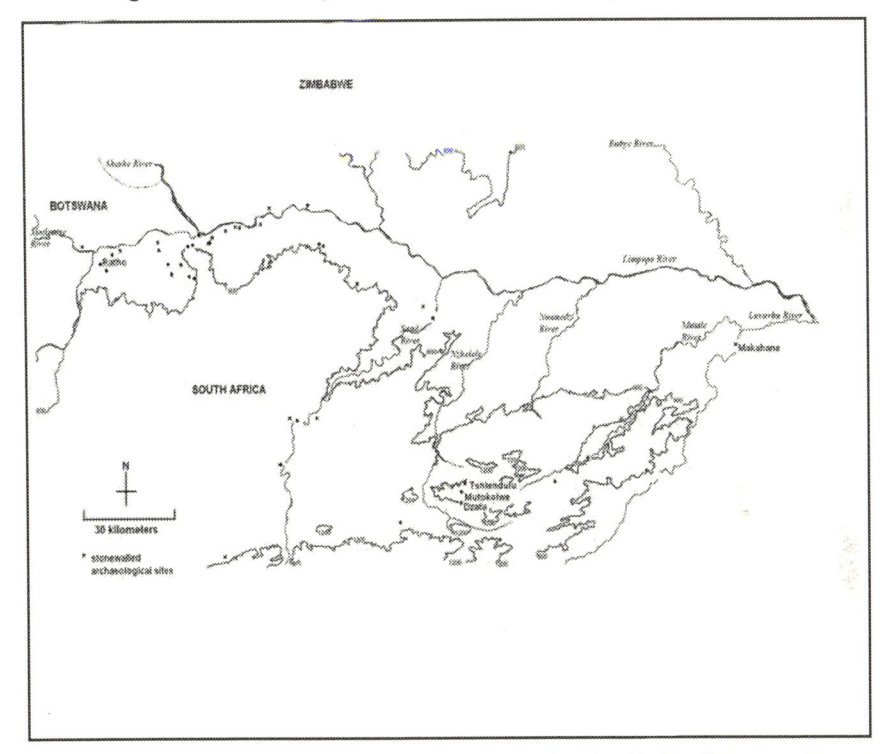

Map 2. The Distribution of Stonewalled Sites Associated with Pre-European Karanga, Rozvi and Venda Speakers on the Southern Zimbabwe Plateau and the Adjacent Northern Regions of South Africa.

SOURCE: Modified from Huffman and Hanisch (1987).

A number of archaeological sites in the Limpopo Province have been excavated by archaeologists. Mapungubwe and Bambandyanalo (K2) on the confluence of the Shashe and Limpopo rivers have a history of intensive excavation going back to the early 1930s (Eloff 1979; Fouche 1937; Gardner 1955 and 1963; Meyer 1998). Although excavation yields archaeological evidence necessary for interpreting the past— and which evidence may be curated for present and future scientific research and other purposes— it destroys the sites concerned. To minimise site destruction, the archaeological deposits and associated structures need stabilisation. Minimally, archaeologists often backfill their excavation trenches— a suitable stabilisation method— and proceed to record the results of their work in considerable detail (see for example, Meyer 1998). However, the scars created by prolonged and extensive site excavation are indelible, especially when viewed from the air. Some past investigators were not able to backfill their trenches, having thrown the soil down the precipice. This is how such sites were left exposed, mostly to the vagaries of the weather, which include short thundershowers, rapid runoff, and gully erosion. In some instances, existing conservation programmes were disrupted by the Second World War, the guerrilla war resulting from the opposition to apartheid, or simply ran aground due to limited or lack of funding. Between 2001 and 2003, Bambandyanalo and Mapungubwe received extensive conservation so as to stabilise their cultural deposits (Coen and Hutten 2006). These included backfilling, use of sandbags and covering materials and strengthening of some pathways and routes, to minimise or stop soil erosion. These measures work to various degrees (Figure 1).

Fig. 1. Stabilised Areas of the Southern Terrace of Mapungubwe Hill

(Photo by the Author).

In conserving sites, archaeologists aim towards maintaining their integrity and thus all conservation measures must be reversible, should cause no damage to the archaeological deposits in their original and other related contexts, must have a low or limited visual impact, and provide maximum protection against all forms of erosion (Nienaber and Hutten 2006). This approach must be cost-effective and technically achievable and undemanding. Other sites to have undergone conservation include the stonewalled town of Thulamela, which was totally reconstructed (Meskell 2007).

1.6 Communities in the Research Area

Defining communities or the public is difficult or always unsatisfactory as either term attempts to describe a diverse range of people cross-cutting age, class, ethnicity, gender, religion and other affiliations (Merriman 2004). Minimally, according to Marshall (2002, 215), communities are aggregations of people that "are seldom, if ever, monocultural and are never of one mind." In this research, which is grounded within community or public archaeology, I employ a definition or concept that is broad-based and sociological.

What I regard as descent or descendant communities are those communities ancestrally linked to some of the archaeological sites and cultural landscapes found in the research area. Some of these communities are located within proximity of sites such as Dzata, and are, by this definition, local descent communities. We also have non-local descent communities, who are communities that are linked or claim cultural links to certain archaeological sites, but that live in another location, some distance away" (see Marshall 2002, 216). Some of these sites date from the early first millennium AD while others can be dated to the proto and historical period, loosely defined here as periods remembered by these communities in their traditions. These communities include mostly, the Venda. Their traditional home lies in the northern regions of South Africa generally within and immediately north and south of the well-watered, moist and fertile Soutpansberg mountains. North of this mountain region, the environment is hot and dry. Some of the Venda speakers still live in southern Zimbabwe, and despite modern political boundaries, share close cultural connections with their counterparts in adjacent South Africa. Because they speak what is now referred to as "the Venda language", they should not be viewed as a monolithic ethnic group. Instead, they are a "composite" of culturally different, but related groups or clans.

Venda origins are known from oral traditions (Stayt 1931; Van Warmelo 1932, 1942 and 1960) and archaeology (Hanisch 2008). The Venda or Vhavenda are descendants of many heterogeneous groups and clans such as Vhadau, Vhakwevho, Vhambedzi, Vhafamadi, Vhania, Vhagoni, Vhalea, Vhaluvhu, Vhatavhatsindi, Vhatwanamba (or Twamamba), Vhanzhelele/Vhalembethu, Vhanyai, Vhalaudzi, Masingo and Vhalemba. The Vhadau, Vhakwevho, Vhafamadi, Vhania, Vhagoni, Vhalea and

Vhaluvhu are collectively known as Vhangona. The Vhangona and Vhambedzi are considered the original inhabitants of the land now called Venda, which is part of the Limpopo Province. The Vhatwanamba, Vhanyai, Vhatavhatsindi and Vhalembethu, Masingo and Vhalaudzi (Vhasenzi) and Vhalemba settled in Venda in the late 1500s. The land of Vhangona was later settled by Karanga-Rozvi clans from Zimbabwe, and the dating of this event is post 1700 AD (Beach 1980). They briefly conquered the Venda and set up a state ruled by the Singo dynasty.

The Venda chiefs are traditionally custodians of the land for their people, while local headmen permit household groups to occupy and work tracts of land. Lineages of kinsmen, with membership based on patrilineal descent, are used to reckon inheritance and succession. Cattle are given as bridewealth. Matrilineal descent is also observed by the Venda, especially in the religious practice of the ancestor cult. Ancestral spirits, including those of chiefs, are among those thought to inhabit the Venda countryside.

In the research area, you also find another kind of local communities living "either on or close to a site". These are usually non-descent local communities, who are not ancestrally related to the site. This category includes landowners and local stakeholders with economic interests in the area such as miners. These non-descent communities have impelled the need for community archaeology. They have also put under severe scrutiny the role of archaeology in the area because of colonial land ownership and recent land claims by some descendant communities. Thus, non-descendant communities are crucial for archaeologists seeking a working knowledge of the area since they provide the much needed access to the sites, the evidence on which archaeologists base their interpretations.

One community or public I want to mention here in passing, but of relevance to the research area is the state or government of South Africa. This is considered 'public' because of what government does 'in the public interest'. Very often tensions arise between the state and local communities. In the research area, Government is represented at various levels, but mainly through the Department of Environmental Affairs and Tourism (DEAT), under which is the South African National Parks (SANParks), the managing authority of Mapungubwe and other nature reserves in the area.

1.7 Organization of This Work

This work is organised in seven chapters. Chapter two explores community or public archaeologies in southern Africa and makes an assessment of why engagement with local and descendant communities should characterise postcolonial approaches in understanding the past. The third chapter details the various methods used in the study. Chapter four presents the data gathered in the field, while Chapter five gives a qualitative analysis of the research findings. Some interpretation of archaeology in the context of communities' understanding of cultural heritage and heritage conservation, and uses of archaeological sites in the present is attempted in Chapter six. The final chapter explores the subject of archaeological relevance and how sharing of archaeological and other relevant cultural knowledge enhances the protection of heritage.

In conducting this project, I am aware that archaeology is not just an exercise in recovering a lost and distant past. Instead, archaeology should be empowering people to engage with that past in a way that is beneficial to their lives in the present. Gone are the days when archaeologists were revered for 'discovering' 'ancient' objects and sharing their exploits to amazed audiences, who were also prepared to listen to archaeologists' storyline of the pasts they investigated. This approach has received serious challenges recently as it became evident that one cannot isolate the past from the present. The new challenge for archaeologists is to involve local and indigenous communities in a process of constructive engagement through a variety of ways, including presentation of heritage sites and fieldwork. It has been demonstrated elsewhere in the world that archaeology can be a useful partnership between us— the professionals — and the people archaeologists engage with. Local communities constitute an important knowledge base, and how professionals process such knowledge and communicate it beyond the confines of our disciplinary boundaries will redefine the nature and character of archaeology in post-colonial southern Africa.

CHAPTER TWO

Communities, Engaging Archaeologies and Heritage Conservation: Definitions, Issues, Challenges and Possibilities

2.1 Introduction

The opening statement of the Venice Charter— the International Charter on the Conservation and Restoration of Monuments and Sites— says in part: "People are becoming more and more conscious of the unity of human values and regard ancient monuments as a common heritage. The common responsibility to safeguard them for future generations is recognised...." (Petzet 2004, 7).

Articles 6 and 7 of the Charter state: "...Whenever the traditional setting exists, it must be kept.... A monument is inseparable from the history to which it bears witness and from the setting in which it occurs...."

The main concern for the Venice Charter is the preservation and conservation of sites and monuments, including "modest works of the past", later defined as cultural heritage, in terms of their authentic fabric. This is achieved, according to the Charter, through recourse to all sciences and techniques of architectural heritage. Emphasis is also given to documentation, which must be conducted during all stages of the conservation, restoration and excavation.

In this study, I use the term conservation and preservation interchangeably, but very loosely to imply protection of archaeological heritage, not only in the limited scientific sense, but also in the spiritual and symbolic sense. According to Petzet (2004), to conserve basically means to preserve. However, there is a broad range of terms such as restoration, renovation, replacement, maintenance, repair, stabilisation, rehabilitation, modernisation, and reconstruction, which may also be used in the same broad context. The terms converge and interconnect with each other to the extent that they constitute what Petzet (2004) refers to as a "graduated system of preservation measures". It is possible to conduct each of these simultaneously or one after the other. The process or measures involve the exchange or replacement of elements or components in or on a site, structure or monument. In archaeological sites or historical buildings, some of these components are historical documents, and as such may only need restoration or copies and not replacement. The archaeological sites described in this study have been subjected to some form of maintenance, repair, rebuilding, stabilisation and reconstruction (Nienaber and Hutten 2006; Meskell 2007) as part of a long-term programme in their conservation. Repair work often occurs at considerable intervals, and is necessitated by inadequate or lack of maintenance. It often refers to the careful and localised exchange of material components.

Because some sites are connected with the present, archaeologists are seeking to engage local communities and their participation as a means of promoting the maintenance of such archaeological heritage. In southern Africa, this principle is especially important when dealing with the heritage directly connected to some indigenous peoples or local ethnic groups. During the past three decades, researchers have provided evidence to support the notion that the social environment in which people live, as well as their lifestyles can influence the incidence of heritage protection within a population (Meskell 2007; Ndoro 2001). They have also demonstrated that a population can achieve long-term heritage protection when people become involved in their community and work together to effect change (Fontein 2006). In view of these findings, historical archaeologists and heritage practitioners in southern Africa are now expanding their efforts to create positive environments and strong community action and influencing public policy in ways that encourage community collaboration (Mgijima and Buthelezi 2006). This thinking about heritage management makes an important departure from colonial approaches that sought to ostracize cultural heritage from the people closely associated with it (Fontein 2006; Ndoro 2001).

Stemming from this renewed emphasis in cultural heritage management, heritage professionals and community leaders can envision many new opportunities to engage people. For example, the use of community collaborations to prevent destruction, rather than relying solely on law enforcement, is a strategy gaining widespread acceptance. The various field reports sponsored by ICCROM, ICOMOS, Africa 2009, CRATerre-EAG, Getty, etc., are testimony to this development. Many of these consist of best practice projects which were initiated in Africa in recent years (see Joffroy 2005; Ndoro 2005; Ndoro and Pwiti 2005; Ndoro, Mumma and Abungu 2008). At the same time though, those working in this field have to confront a number of pragmatic issues. One of these issues is how to integrate this vision of community engagement into corporate or academic approaches to doing business (see Odora-Hoppers 2002). Besides, the heritage professional, community organizer, or volunteer who sees promise in addressing the social environment as a means of promoting heritage may find it necessary to convince others of the usefulness of a particular community-level approach.

To some extent, this study in cultural heritage conservation is also about what individuals and communities choose to remember or memorialise. Heritage is the things from the past which people consider worth conserving and memorialising, while memory is the selective recall of significant cultural values and practices. Closer to memory is identity construction, where identities are the self-definitions which individuals and groups construct for themselves and which heritage and memory have helped to shape. These intricate and intersecting processes of heritage, memory and identity are increasingly becoming a focus of academic study (Anheier and Isar 2011). What may be relevant here with regards to the Venda as a subject of this study is their membership of various social or more specifically clan groups that are continuously in the process of self-making and sense-making of the world around them, and how influential individuals within these clans draw strength from community kinship, religious and class affiliation and help people acquire, localise and recall their memories, heritage and identities (see Halbwachs 1980 and 1992). Perhaps, this is how the Venda cultural landscape has been shaped – through the day-to-day practices of memorial construction of how the past is manifest in the present.

Linked with the issue of memory is the invention of pasts or traditions (see Hobsbawm 1983; Hobsbawm and Ranger 1983). According to Michael Kammen (1991), societies reconstruct their pasts rather than faithfully record them, and they do so with the needs of contemporary culture in mind, manipulating their pasts in order to shape the present. The qualification and identity of being descent is very much contentious, as this is something internal to the communities claiming such links with the past and assumed identities.

Using examples from around the globe, this chapter presents the theoretical frame of community or public archaeology as understood and practiced at the moment. This takes the form of a literature review. It also discusses the concept of 'community' and its meanings and relevance in a cultural heritage context. The chapter winds up by contextualising public or community archaeology or archaeologies as practiced in Africa, suggesting the nature of engagement that is relevant to them.

2.2 Defining Communities

The term 'community' is a fluid concept, which is quite problematic in terms of definition and application in the fields of archaeology and more broadly in the spheres of cultural heritage management. What a heritage practitioner refers to as 'community' may not match another's definition (Kretzmann and McKnight 1993). However, those interested in working with a community must first have a clear picture of the entity they are trying to address. Understanding the dimensions of the concept of community enables those initiating engagement processes to better target their efforts and work with community leaders and members in developing appropriate engagement strategies. Overall, archaeologists have realised that the terms 'community archaeology' and 'community heritage' remain fundamentally underdeveloped. While notions of 'community archaeology' and 'community heritage' have become increasingly prevalent in recent times, I would like to suggest here that these terms, and indeed their philosophical underpinnings, remain significantly underdeveloped. Key to this underdevelopment is a fetishisation of material artefacts (see Riley and Harvey 2005), which works to obscure and truncate a range of intangible values, experiences and encounters tied up with any engagement with heritage and the past. Maintaining this privileged position of 'materiality' lends legitimacy and primacy to archaeological expertise, encouraging a communicative relationship between 'expert' and 'community' groups that are defined by a repressed dialogicality. Consequently, 'community' heritage and archaeology projects have in many instances become synonymous with the rhetoric of 'trowel fodder' (Riley and Harvey 2005). Rather than an engaged and collaborative conversation, the relationship is dominated by instruction and the passing of information one-way, to which community groups are encouraged to react (Greer, Harrison, and McIntyre-Tamwoy 2002). Subsequently within this communicative flow, community groups and individuals are constructed and sustained as active participants only in relation to a more powerful agent— the archaeological expert.

Already, archaeologists are unhappy with the recent 'cult of community' as proposed by McClanahan (2007), and adopted elsewhere. Foremost, it intends to take account of the complex personal, social and political relationships underpinning community collaborations, not only within the community, but those between community groups and notions of 'expertise', which are traditionally haunted by distrust, suspicion and unease.[1] This project views community in broader sociological or systems perspective (see for example Kretzmann and McKnight 1993), where the term refers to a group of people united by at least one common characteristic, e.g. geography, shared interests, values, experiences, politics, or traditions. Central to the definition of a community is a sense of inclusion as well as exclusion from membership. Thus an individual may be a member of a community by choice, as or by virtue of their innate personal characteristics, such as age, gender, race, or ethnicity. As a result, individuals may belong to multiple communities at any one time. These complex associations are critical in understanding community dynamics in any part of the world. In southern Africa identities are based on communities largely defined along ethic lines, but these constructs are also problematic as some were constructed by the apartheid regime as a divide and rule tactic (Hall 1984).

The research adopts a working definition of community engagement, viewed here as the process of working collaboratively with and through groups of people affiliated by geographic proximity, special interest, or similar situations to address issues affecting the well-being of those people. It is an avenue for restoring cultural heritage rights lost following land alienation. Community is first defined by history, then ethnicity and geographical contingency. This is the basis for traditional, indigenous knowledge, which has been accumulated over three or more centuries

---

[1] See comments in the various session abstracts of the *World Archaeological Congress*, Dublin, 29 June-4 July 2008, e.g. http://www.ucd.ie/wac-6/programme/45.html [accessed 8 February 2008]

among the Venda and neighbouring Sotho, Shona, and Tswana groups, which this research seeks to acquire in order to inform conservation of the capitals or residences of their kings and other important settlements.

Minimally, communities are aggregations of people that "are seldom, if ever, monocultural and are never of one mind" (Kretzmann and McKnight 1993; McClanahan 2007). Public archaeologists generally use a working definition that broadly categorizes communities into three types. Even so, there is considerable overlap and convergence. Thus, you have local communities, local descent communities, and non-local descent communities (Marshall 2002 and 2009).

Descent communities would be defined as those with ancestral connections to a particular cultural landscape, or specific archaeological site. These communities can be considered local if they live within the proximity of the cultural landscape or site they are ancestrally connected to, or non-local descent communities if they now live in another geographical location. In southern Africa, non-local descent communities are perhaps in the majority given the complicated histories of pre-European migrations (for the Zimbabwe plateau and adjacent lowlands including the research area, (see Beach 1980; Ralushai and Gray 1977) and European land possessions leading to forced removals. The Venda and other groups are claiming ancestral connections with and ownership of some of the sites in this study (Tshimangadzo, forthcoming). Recently, collaboration with archaeologists has culminated in the conservation of some of these sites. The stabilization of the archaeological deposits at Mapungubwe and Bambandyanalo, the re-construction of the stone walls at Thulamela, and reburial of human remains excavated from Mapungubwe and other sites nearby are key examples. There have also been consultations with some of the communities on the proposed mining of coal in an area perceived as a threat to the Mapungubwe Cultural Landscape. Further consultations with communities are necessary due to land claims by some Venda clans, as this has a bearing on future management of the cultural landscape. In this study, the entity 'Venda' as community or communities is unpacked to show their diversity and heterogeneity both diachronically and synchronically (see Chapter one). This is important because, as is shown in Chapter four, even the concept 'Venda' lends itself to an invented tradition, in particular for land claim purposes and recognition during the 'official' reburial rituals of the human remains from Mapungubwe.

Because of the historical developments just mentioned, the research area is also populated by non-descent local communities. Most Europeans have carved out large commercial farms in the Limpopo Province, a colonization process that impacted on a number of archaeological sites. The creation of the Dongola Botanical Reserve in 1922 specifically for the study of the vegetation and assessing the agricultural potential of the area is part of the broader land alienation process that ostracized local descent communities from their cultural landscapes, and at the same time created a new type of local community— communities that lived either on or close to known archaeological sites and/or cultural landscapes with no direct cultural connection or ancestry to such places. As aforementioned, some of these 'lost ancestral lands' have now been re-claimed by local descent communities. The current socio-political context of land-redistribution and management of natural and cultural resources revolves around the relationship between residential, non-descent communities and non-local descent communities. As will be shown later in this work, conservation of existing sites and cultural landscapes is not just about sustainable use of resources, but also (re)connections with traditional, in this case, descent communities.

The other community that may be included here is the 'stakeholder', who may not be local in terms of residence or descent, but has a vested interest in the management or administration of a given landscape. Mining companies, wildlife management authorities, municipal authorities, or even the state or government are defined in this work as such.

2.3 Literature Review

In this section, I present an overview of community and public archaeologies as practiced in different parts of the world outside the African continent. In general, these are archaeologies where interactions and collaborations with 'indigenous' peoples are critical for their success. Indigenous peoples have a keen interest in the material remains of the past and in the intellectual understanding, construction and use of their cultures, identities, and intangible and tangible heritage. Over the last few decades, the indigenous populations the world over have become increasingly engaged in the theory and practice of archaeology, and increasingly vocal about issues of sovereignty and cultural heritage, as part of a concerted effort to gain control over archaeological and political uses of their past (Bruchac, Hart, and Wobst 2010; for South Africa, see Mafune 2010; Ndlovu 2010). In this study, I problematize the word indigenous because the term assumes a totally different meaning when used in Africa. The term 'indigenous' in Africa mostly refers to those groups of people who have been living by hunting and gathering and by migratory nomadic pastoralism. It also refers to those peoples practicing traditional drylands horticulture including oasis cultures. Indigeneity is associated with both the negative experience of discrimination and marginalisation from governance, as well as the positive aspects of being holders of unique knowledge which has emerged through the long-term management of arid area and tropical forest ecosystems. Indigenous cultures arise and are sustained by the wise use of natural resources (see http://www.ipacc.org.za/eng/who.asp). In this work, I prefer using the term communities, but specifically referring to archaeologists' relationships with local, descent communities, in contexts where they have encountered the practice of archaeology in one way or the other, but have not reached the stage where they have been able to direct or conduct research projects themselves.

According to Marshall (2002), Australia has a lengthy history of community archaeology, with research projects involving collaboration between archaeologists and aboriginal groups akin to archaeologists in North America collaborating with American Indians, First Peoples and other groups (see in the following presentation). Cultural landscapes such as Ukuru (Ayers Rock) are now wholly managed by local descent communities (see Layton 2001).

There are numerous examples of public or community archaeology in Canada and the United States of America (Kerber 2006). These have generally taken the form of research projects that involve and engage native Indian populations and other local and descendant communities. There are also projects that involve public outreach or education.

Collaboration with the American Indians has been conditioned by the long history of white American archaeologists excavating native sites including burial, collecting artefacts and human remains from them (Watkins 2003). Interpretation by these archaeologists of local material culture and production of knowledge regarding the native American Indian past has also been a bone of contention. Furthermore, the introduction of a system aimed at protecting Indian American cultural heritage was confronted with distrust. North American archaeology involving indigenous or 'First Peoples' has changed in terms of thrust and emphasis, highlighted by engagement and collaboration. According to Kerber (2006),

> . . . archaeology benefits American Indians and First People of Canada, respectively, by contributing important historical information; assisting in land claims; managing cultural resources and burial for protection from current and future impacts; promoting sovereignty; offering employment opportunities through field work, interpretive centers, and tourism; educating the young; aiding in nation (re-) building and self-discovery; demonstrating innovative responses of past groups to changing environmental and social circumstance; and providing populations themselves with skills and experience in doing archaeology. Clearly, collaborative archaeology is not a panacea for the difficulties facing indigenous groups, but in certain situations . . . it can be a powerful tool.

Some scholars would contest this claim, arguing that collaboration with American Indians is only new "from the perspective of the dominant culture" (Dean and Perelli 2006) and that "American Indians have been cooperating and collaborating with their neighbours and visitors for hundreds of years. Others point to the problem arising as a result of American federal government recognizing some as bona-fide tribes or communities and not others (Watkins 2003 and 2006). Some of these communities are claiming human remains to be repatriated to their communities (Blume 2006).

Outside the American Indians, some public archaeology projects in North America involve local communities, descent communities and descent diasporas (Singleton and Orser 2003). A major aim of some of these projects is to recover and present forgotten aspects of race relations in local communities as contained in the histories of slavery and experiences of racial segregation (Shackel 2007). A general aspect of archaeology which intersects with the public takes the form of outreach through museum displays, and researchers presenting their work in schools, and through the public media. The idea is to 'educate' the public about the past, so that its relevance is appreciated (Blume 2006).

Although the term public or community archaeology is rarely used in the United Kingdom (Liddle 1985), countries like Australia have a long tradition of community archaeology, going back to the late 19th century. The reasons for this are evident from the antiquarian interests of people like General Pitt Rivers. The UK also has a long history of volunteer involvement in archaeological projects, some of whom the volunteers initiated. It appears though that community or public archaeology is fast disappearing, and urgent guidelines are needed from English Heritage, the Council for British Archaeology and other relevant bodies on how to define the future for community or public archaeology. Faulkner (2000) argues that general volunteerism, as well as public participation or involvement, seems to have been constrained by UK legislation, such as requirements of the Planning Policy Guidance note 16 (PPG16) and the full professionalization of archaeological practice. Apart from this, participation has also been sidelined or diminished by development-driven commercial, mainly contract, archaeology.

The author's knowledge of community archaeology in mainland Europe is very sketchy. A major challenge to public participation seems to be the European Convention on the Protection of the Archaeological Heritage of 1992 (the Valletta Convention), which states that all archaeological work should be carried out by suitably qualified, authorized people. This article effectively 'licensed' archaeologists in mainland Europe and the UK (which ratified the Convention in 2001) to do the work which, in the past, could also be done by voluntary archaeologists and local societies.

2.4 Archaeology in the Eyes of Communities in Africa

There are very few cited examples of public or community archaeology on the African continent. However, archaeologists practicing in Africa now see the imperative in consulting local communities in doing their work. This work can vaguely be considered public archaeology, but rather, an attempt by archaeologists to make their work more acceptable in the public domain. The most informative publication that captures this view is Mapunda and Lane (2004), arguing that archaeological engagement with the public in eastern Africa has had very little impact. This is largely due to the failure by archaeologists, museums and other interpretive centres to effectively communicate the discipline to the public. The authors point out that the level of site presentation and interpretation is also poor.

Engaging local communities in archaeology is an exercise that goes hand in hand with cultural heritage promotion and protection. In southern Africa, this approach is especially important when dealing with the heritage of indigenous peoples or local ethnic groups. During the past three decades, researchers in the region have provided evidence to support the notion that the social environment in which people live, as well as their lifestyles can influence the incidence of heritage protection within a population (Meskell 2007; Ndoro 2001). They have also demonstrated that a population can achieve long-term heritage protection when people become involved in their community and work together to effect change (Fontein 2006). In view of these findings, heritage practitioners in southern Africa are now expanding their efforts to create positive environments and strong community action, and influencing public policy in ways that encourage community collaboration (Mgijima and Buthelezi 2006). This thinking about heritage management is an important departure from colonial approaches that sought to ostracize cultural heritage from the people closely associated with it (Fontein 2006; Ndoro 2001).

It is important to communicate to communities why participation and engagement is worthwhile. The processes for involvement and participation must be appropriate to meet the overall goals and objectives of the engagement (see Matowanyika 2000; Bicker *et al.* 2004). In southern Africa, the tendency has been to put in place some legislative requirements as condition or framework for community involvement in cultural heritage projects. However, the parameters for community engagement should be initially defined by the need to enhance access to cultural heritage resources which have been "fenced off" from communities as a result of colonial legislation or apartheid land alienation. This work reports that regardless of how much knowledge archaeologists may have about a particular site or place, consultations and guidance from local descendant communities is imperative for the success of a conservation project.

2.5 Conclusion

Archaeologists have always struggled to make their work relevant to communities within which they operate. So should African archaeologists act as catalysts of Western science and local knowledge, and if so, what messages should they be communicating in this regard? Local communities are unlikely to pay attention towards any profession or discipline that is not likely to benefit them, especially in a world characterised by lack of access to basic amenities, poverty, underdevelopment, conflict and violence. Instead, archaeologists must be prepared to broaden their knowledge base by incorporating traditional or local wisdom. These engaged and useful archaeologies attempt to address and inform these problems by reshaping the structure of academic communication with communities of indigenous people, descendant communities, and researchers from other disciplines. They also have the potential to recast the roles and responsibilities of archaeologists to the communities in and with which they work. They recognize the voices of indigenous groups, descendant communities, and other constituencies, ensuring that they possess power within the whole course of the archaeological process. They also provide relevant, useful and timely information which can serve as a tool for solving social and scientific problems.

Such approaches to archaeology, as called for by a wide section of the global community (see Atalay [Ojibwe] 2007), act as an effective foil for intellectual colonialism. In doing so, they cast researchers as facilitators who have something to offer in exchange for the archaeological information that they collect and helps to balance the complex power relationships between researchers and communities. Ultimately, archaeology becomes a tool for civic engagement, activism, and social justice as well as a powerful source of information about the history of the human race and the world it inhabits (Shackel 2007).

Engaged archaeologies can lead towards community rebuilding and healing. Reburial of human skeletal remains excavated by archaeologists in the Mapungubwe Cultural Landscape should be viewed as an acknowledgement of the importance of local indigenous values, which in turn are central to cultural landscape preservation. Reburial of the human remains restores some dignity to communities who feel they have been 'wronged' by the actions of archaeologists, and also restores cultural values to the associated landscape.

There are other conservation programmes in the research area. Current scientific approaches in site conservation in parts of the Limpopo Province are well covered in Nienaber and Hutten (2006) but there are virtually no publications on the re-construction of the stonewalled sites such as Dzata and Thulamela.

Beyond Mapungubwe and Bambandyanalo, preservation and conservation is on the settings around these sites—the 'physical environment' that makes up the current Mapungubwe National Park. Despite serious archaeological research (Huffman 2000, 2005 and 2007), this setting is for aesthetic appreciation (Figs. 2 and 3) as well as for the interpretation of the cultural landscape and the 'experience' created by visitors coming to the place.

Fig. 2. Some of the Breathtaking Scenery of the Mapungubwe Cultural Landscape (Photo by the author).

To many descendant local communities, settings consist of both visual and non-visual elements, the latter encompassing the spiritual connections to place (see, Mairi 2005). To the ordinary tourist, settings are primarily visual, although the spiritual aspects are welcome in contributing to the experience of visiting the place (see also Colcutt 1999).

Fig. 3. View of the Shashe-Limpopo Confluence

(Photo by the author)

To the management authority, which is South African National Parks (SANParks), this setting is now part of biodiversity. Biodiversity is generally defined as the variety of life, the different plants, animals and micro-organisms, their genes and the ecosystems of which they are part. However, it is now generally difficult to discuss biodiversity without taking into account the human element, because of the way humans have influenced the broader environment. Human culture and bio-diversity should therefore not be regarded as separate entities but an integral part of the same process as both create relationships with the ecosystem.

CHAPTER THREE

Approaches to Community Archaeology in the Limpopo Province, South Africa

3.1 Introduction

One of the issues raised in the previous chapter is whether South African archaeology in particular or southern African archaeology in general is community-based or -oriented, or whether it is primarily academic, dominated by a few, and reactive to the dictates of legislation. This chapter is written in this context, arguing that current approaches in archaeology are still 'academic' and 'development-driven'. However, there is room for community archaeology to take centre stage and drive future directions in archaeology if archaeologists change their approaches in dealing with communities. Current approaches are rooted in 'traditional' archaeology, an enquiry-based science, with the objective of finding empirical 'truths', and whose findings must be published in academic journals or books, or presented as reports for modern developers. The only community interface with archaeology is the occasional encounter with the museum or interpretive centre, but these too are problematic in matters of archaeological site or heritage interpretation and representation.

A number of approaches to community archaeology include those that relegate the interpretation of the bulk of the material evidence to archaeologists (Atalay 2006 and 2007; Marshall 2002), those that employ a degree of ethnographic knowledge in dealing with communities (Pyburn 2003 and 2009), participatory action research (Pyburn 2007), and, popular dissemination of archaeological knowledge (Atalay 2006). Cutting across all these is the conviction that long-term relationships are necessary to develop a rapport and mutual respect with local communities, since to attain successful collaboration, archaeologists must make a long-term commitment in order to understand the dynamics of the social context of their research. My experience with the archaeology of the research area demonstrates that all these approaches are possible to varying degrees, and play a pivotal role in the engagement process whose objective is to make the work of archaeologists relevant among the communities in which they work.

I discuss some of the research methods and approaches employed in this study. It is apparent that in most forms of archaeological practice, museum display or heritage experience will contain and represent an engagement of some kind with the 'relevant' community. This was not the main objective here, but rather, to determine what is relevant in a given community context.

3.2 Research Design

This research was conceived within the framework of what we refer to at the University of Pretoria as basic social sciences; and therefore, relevant research methods in social sciences were used (see Babbie 1998; Bless and Higson-Smith 2000). The research was structured in a number of components in an attempt to address core research questions (Denzin and Lincoln 2011). A research design refers to the strategies used to inquire about the topic of interest and the individuals as well as the instruments used in data collection (Creswell 2003; Nachmias and Nachmias 1981). My background training in archaeology as a social science in the context of the broader humanities also dictated that I follow sequences of stages that guide the conduct of archaeological research or investigations. Although a number of sites are mentioned in this research, I did not follow site-oriented research as is the practice in traditional archaeology where sites are excavated, artefacts collected, described in detail and analysed for the production of an excavation report. It is the conduct of traditional archaeology and its consequences that is problematized by this research. I followed archaeological research design as described by Ashmore and Sharer (2009).

Ethical considerations

Matters of cultural heritage are sensitive (Renzetti and Lee 1993) as they have potential consequences or implications either directly or indirectly for participants or even the researchers. The research concerned can be controversial. In this context, my research was considered sensitive in matters dealing with or verging on the sacred, and the communities' sensitivities towards heritage places and human remains and burials were taken into account.

To protect the participants who took part in the research, a number of ethical considerations were taken into account. This research received clearance from SANParks, the management authority of the Mapungubwe Cultural Landscape. In Venda, where oral interviews were conducted, we applied the principle of voluntary participation whereby our participants were not coerced to be involved with our research. The participants were further requested orally about the nature of the research being conducted and the risks that could arise as a result of their participation. This research was conducted in the contexts of a number of highly politicised developments in the research area linked to the land-claims as well the mining within culturally sensitive zones adjacent to the Mapungubwe Cultural Landscape. The participants understood these and gave their consent to participate in the oral interviews. This research also ensured that participants were not placed at risk of psychological and physical harm by clearly informing them of the intellectual objectives of the research. Participants were also given the assurance that their research would be treated in confidence, and that the information generated from the research would not be made available to anyone without their informed, written or oral consent. To guarantee privacy of participants, the researcher adhered to the principle of anonymity as required by the University of Pretoria Research and Ethics Committee as well as the ethical standards prescribed by SANParks and within the general social sciences in South Africa. The ethical standards as underlined by OSSREA in their grant-holder contract agreement were also adhered to. Fundamentally, the research did not treat participants as 'experimental objects'.

Beyond these institutional requirements, the research treated the participants with all due respect as expected in Venda custom. Knowledge from these people, particularly elders who are sometimes regarded as 'moving libraries', is always imbued with wisdom, and ultimately represents a learning experience on the part of the researcher (see Setlhabi 2010). Thus, the researcher is a participant in as much as he or she is an observer when gathering and collating of oral data and ethnography.

Since this research is an investigation of whether there is a platform for community-based or public archaeology in southern Africa, the research had to be grounded in cultural heritage studies. The proliferation of cultural heritage studies in the last decade leads to the assumption that there are research methods in place in addressing issues arising in the subject. Apparently, this was not the case. The research instruments detailed in the following section present a general sequence in which the research was structured and for which this research report is an outcome (see also Pikirayi 2007, 2011).

3.3 Population of the Study

The population of the study was restricted to communities from Venda, with a specific interest on the world heritage site of Mapungubwe and a general interest in Venda origins and clan histories. This population was conceived within the context of a pool for which information was gathered to address the research questions. The pool included the following:

i. Community or clan members, in their individual capacities, mainly from Venda, who participated in oral interviews, presenting views on cultural heritage protection, the repatriation and the reburial exercises.

ii. Community or clan representatives who attended meetings with stakeholders (the University of Pretoria; the Department of Environmental Affairs and Tourism and South African National Parks [SANParks]) for the repatriation of human remains to Mapungubwe.

iii. Communities in a collective capacity and/or community or clan leaders, the latter who spoke about or commented on the repatriation process during the symbolic handover, cleansing and reburial ceremonies.

3.4 Data Gathering Instruments and Approaches

3.4.1 Archaeological Fieldwork

A number of visits were made to archaeological sites selected for detailed study. One site – Bambandyanalo (K2), an extensive midden— lays within the Mapungubwe Cultural Landscape (MCL); another is located in a farm called Ratho, and Dzata is found in the heart of Venda. The latter two are stonewalled structures. Mapungubwe Hill, the 13th century capital of an ancient kingdom, was not studied per se, but referred to on matters of repatriation and restitution. Originally, I intended to include Makahane and other stonewalled sites and although site visits were made, no further investigations were made due to logistical and financial reasons.

Condition surveys were conducted at the only stone structure located in Ratho Farm (Figure 4), and at Bambandyanalo (Figure 5), immediately south of the Shashe-Limpopo confluence and this involved some kind of documentation. Cultural heritage professionals are putting emphasis on documentation, and this seems to be the developing trend during the last two decades or more.

Fig. 4. The Stonewalled Site in Ratho Farm, Middle Limpopo Valley
Photo by the author.

Fig. 5. The Archaeological Site of Bambandyanalo Showing Vegetation Growing on the
Central Settlement Area. The Ridge Stretching to the Background Is Regarded
as the Central Midden (Photo courtesy of Johan Nel).

Conservation of cultural heritage requires a critical understanding of the significance, condition, and complexity of a place and documentation is critical in attaining this. Documentation is regarded as a critical part of the conservation planning process and something that provides a long-term foundation for the monitoring, maintenance, and management of a site or cultural landscape. The documentation must be done properly to ensure the production of good reliable and usable records, as these ensure that knowledge of heritage places will be passed on to future generations (see Letellier 2007).

According to Letellier (2007) the documentation of built heritage places, must be strengthened. In other words, existing documentation on a given heritage place should be supplemented by a wide range of documentation techniques to match the conservation needs of the sites or cultural landscapes one is working on. This does not necessarily have to involve high-tech gadgetry, as long as the objective is to produce sufficient or adequate heritage information for purposes of conservation, and ultimately, managing the site. Documentation must also be continuous since it is the basis for the monitoring, management, and routine maintenance of a site and provides a way to transmit knowledge about heritage places to future generations.

The world is confronted with serious cultural and even natural heritage losses arising from natural and human-made disasters, modern development, wars and other forms of human conflict. This is compounded by poor or inappropriate conservation. Because of this, and the reality that we cannot save all cultural and other forms of heritage at risk or facing destruction, documentation is one way of doing so before losses are incurred. This is the basis for which subsequent conservators and the future generation will come to know what was there and what efforts were made to save the heritage. According to Letellier (2007), recording is "a prerequisite for informed conservation...[and] a prime responsibility of everybody involved....

Condition assessments are management tools for cultural heritage places, and are critical in assessing conservation needs (Ndoro 2001). Heritage managers and archaeologists work on the assumption that archaeological sites and heritage places are in theory protected by the law, though there are variations in terms of degree on the nature of the protection. Some sites receive better protection than others; some are protected informally, while others are not protected at all. In Africa, standards of the conservation of cultural heritage places are defined or set by Africa 2009 (see *Project Cadre* http://www.africa2009.net/common/reports/botsw03.pdf). In general, when conducting condition surveys or assessments, we are looking at the levels of damage or degradation and making attempts to minimize the problem.

Condition surveys assist in informing us about principles of site construction, restoration and maintenance, thus bridging the gap between the past and the present. There is need to tally this with aspects of community life and local belief systems. This is demonstrated by Onjala and Kamaru (2005) in the case of the stonewalled site of Thimlich Ohinga in the Nyanza Province of Kenya. They show that traditional conservation practices were embedded within a complex social system. The stonewalls were an extension of society, since they provided protection from outside attack. To protect the site and ensure that the walls were not destroyed, a number of taboos were established to govern the conduct of society when using and interacting with the structures. Linkages with the ancestral world were emphasised. These taboos continued to operate even after total abandonment of the site in the early 20th century. For purposes of maintenance and repair, the site was regularly inspected, monitored, its structural problems assessed, labour and resource mobilisation involving the resident community led by traditional experts, elders and the chief. The annual maintenance of the mud-walled Na-Yiri palace of Kokologho in Burkina Fasso is linked to a customary festival of Na-Basga, which mobilises the residential community weeks in advance, and presents an opportunity to pass knowledge from elders to young people, maintain social cohesion, and respect for forgotten customs and values (Rakatomamonjy and Napon 2005).

3.4.2 Archaeological Ethnography

Archaeological ethnography is generally, the introduction of ethnographic methods into archeological projects, or the merging of ethnographic and archaeological practices in order to explore the contemporary relevance and meaning of the archaeological past for diverse publics, the politics of archaeological practice, the claims and contestations involving past material traces and landscapes. The term arises from the realization that indigenous people and other groups are contesting or challenging the results of archaeology; reflexivity as the key theoretical feature of archaeology; the realization that archaeology is a social practice in the present; the proliferation of archaeologies of heritage and studies on the socio-politics of archaeology and the material past (Meskell 2007; Hamilakis and Anagnostopoulos 2009).

The term itself is not new, having been introduced in ethnoarchaeology in the 1970s, but is now used to address issues beyond ethnography, ethnohistory and conventional archaeology. It is not a methodology per se. It is a series of practices which are more than a re-introduction of ethnography into archaeological projects. It is also not just about combining and mixing archaeological and ethnographic-anthropological practices. It is practice that provides space for engagement, dialogue, and critique centered upon archaeology and involving researchers and non-researchers.

This research involved the documentation of relevant or appropriate ethnographies during the desktop assessment stage that would inform the importance of archaeological sites to descendant communities. Most of the results are discussed in Chapter six within the context of the reburial of human remains in the Mapungubwe Cultural Landscape. The exercise was also used as a critique of the current usage of ethnography in archaeology, particularly the interpretation of Mapungubwe and Great Zimbabwe phase sites (Huffman 2005 and 2007).

According to Hamilakis and Anagnostopoulos (2009), for archaeological ethnography to succeed, it "will have to dislodge the certainties of archaeology, the belief placed in its absolute authority, and its naturalization by its practitioners as the sole and exclusive agent for the production of discourses and practices about ancient things" (p. 66). In this work, references to archaeological ethnography are used in locating the meaning of cultural heritage to descendant communities. Oral interviews, as well as sentiments of community representatives during the negotiations and the processes resulting in reburial of human remains from Mapungubwe are regarded as such.

3.4.3 Oral Interviews

Oral narratives and oral histories offer ways of reading, interpreting and shaping the past. These histories are in constant process of becoming and operate within fluid parameters that are shaped and shifted by cultural memories, archaeological data and emerging ideologies (Henige 1974 and 1982). Multiple histories can thus co-exist in an unresolved dialectical tension and narrating these histories results in stories of communities in the research area. In conducting oral interviews, I was conscious of the interrelationship between memory, materiality and cultural heritage. This exercise was not about collecting oral traditions (see Vansina 1985) relating to specific Venda heritage places or landscapes (Hanisch 2008; Ralushai and Gray 1977; Van Warmelo 1932 and 1960) or historical documentation of Venda heritage, but an exercise in ascertaining how the past was valued, used and accessed in a particular geographical and cultural context. According to the ethnographic literature, there are many stories, legends and myths about Venda origins. The resultant narratives are all about the nature of the Venda people and their landscape, what these people did and how the present is part of their history. The narratives are so diverse and conflicting that they are impossible to reconcile, even with the help of other sources of evidence (see Hanisch 2008).

The oral interviews conducted for this study were designed to assess the level of descendant community awareness of archaeological heritage in the Limpopo Province. Questions focused on conservation programmes and the involvement of communities in these. The exercise also attempted an understanding of community approaches to cultural heritage conservation and what methods, if any, they preferred as part of their tradition in preserving heritage places. The interviews also attempted to assess levels of community awareness of intangible aspects connected with some heritage places/sites, and their importance in interpreting or understanding the cultural meanings of these places.

Data gathering sessions involved formal interviews with randomly selected participants from Venda as well as some Venda speakers from nearby urban centres who had a keen interest in the subject of archaeological cultural heritage conservation. Interviews were also informally conducted during the reburial ceremonies in the Mapungubwe Cultural Landscape. The Nzhelele Valley, where most Venda people live today, the Kokwane/Gondeni Prehistoric Footprints site, Dzata Ruins, and the urban areas of Thohoyandou and Makhado were the focus of oral interviews. Some of these places ideally provided a cultural context in which the interviews already carried significant social meaning. The Kokwane Footprint site is a hill where stones can be found with animal and human footprints imprinted on them. The site is being developed for tourism as it is stated in Venda legends that animals and humans left these imprints a long time ago when the stones were still soft. The stonewalled site of Dzata is located in the heart of the Nzhelele valley. It was the chief town of the Venda people, which features quite prominently in their history. However, the site remains under-researched. There is need to combine oral, written and archaeological evidence to understand more about the Venda past in this area, which seems to have been settled between AD 1700 and 1750. This settlement is linked with the Singo dynasty, possibly of Rozvi-descent from Zimbabwe, who may have conquered the various Venda clans and united them into what is sometimes referred to as the Thovela state (Huffman 1996). According to oral traditions, the last known or legendary king of this capital shortly before its abandonment was Thohoyandou. The fragmentation of Venda into small independent chiefdoms and the various clans that we see today may date from this period.

Not very far from Dzata is Tshiendulu Mountain, which is associated with two other stonewalled sites, and dating to much earlier settlement in the area. Archaeologists date this event to AD 1435–1550 and AD 1630–1650 (Hanisch 2008; Loubser 1992). These sites are possibly linked to early Venda settlement in the Soutpansberg range of mountains, prior to expansion into the Nzhelele valley. Settlement on Tshiendulu is also associated with the Singo dynasty, and legends link the sites with Dambanyika/Dyambeu Vele Lambeu and his family. Tshiendulu Mountain is regarded as sacred by the Venda (Stayt 1931; van Warmelo 1932 and 1940). Some of the informants interviewed, such as an old woman who did not reveal her age to us, claimed to have lived in some of the settlements near the village of Mabirinisu, dating more than 100 years. The VhaNgona clan of Venda claim these sites belong to their ancestors.

There is some form of management at Dzata and Kokwane, combining both 'Western' forms of cultural heritage conservation with traditional ones. Both sites are manned by heritage managers, who participated in the oral interviews. Around Tshiendulu and Dzata, communities have been prepared for eco-mapping to appreciate the importance of mapping as a tool to recognize past traditional use and occupancy of landscapes such as mountains, forests and agricultural land. Eco-mapping is considered a dynamic and participatory way for communities to learn more about and comprehend their local environment, and landscape. It also provides opportunities for the transfer of traditional ecological/indigenous knowledge from present to future generations (CEG 2007). Such ecological awareness has been an ongoing project in Venda since January 2007 when the first South African Cultural Biodiversity (CB) and Community Ecological Governance (CEG) celebration was held in the Limpopo Province. This was in recognition of primary school students who had built a traditional homestead, and planted indigenous trees and medicinal plants. The elders were also involved, showcasing their household goods and traditional foods. This accorded the younger generation an opportunity to learn more about their elders' material culture and other aspects of Venda traditions. Another place of great importance is Songozwi village, the Royal Court of the Mphephu Ramabulana, some 10 kilometres north of Louis Trichardt or Makhado. In the mountain in which the village is located is a sacred grove where ancestors of the Mphephu Ramabulana, dating from the mid-1700s, are buried. The custodians of the site uphold certain practices for the protection of the vegetation and the graves, a good example of eco-mapping and conservation.

3.4.4 Participatory Action Research (PAR)

This research is also an exercise in action research or participatory action research (PAR) (Cornwall and Jewkes 1995). Some scholars prefer using the term "participatory research" over and above "participatory action research" because, they argue, action research is not as orientated towards social change (e.g. Stoecker 1999) and does not necessarily engage participants directly in the research process (Kindon, Pain and Kesby 2007). The various definitions of PAR reflect that it is more of an approach than a method of inquiry. Generally, PAR involves experimental approaches that focus on the effects of the researcher's direct actions of practice within a participatory community. PAR adopts a very different approach to conventional research in the way it actively engages participants in the research process, from research design to dissemination of information. According to Tolman and Brydon-Miller (2001), PAR challenges scientific approaches to research where focus is on proven 'truths', thus confronting potential bias and subjectivity, quantifying constructs into measurable units, and prediction and control. The objective is to improve the performance quality of the community or an area of concern.

There are various perceptions of PAR (Cahill 2007; Cahill and Torre 2007). PAR is not a theoretical approach, although it generates theory as part of the research outcome. It is an approach or a research process which is context-specific, that puts emphasis on collaboration with researchers and participants working together to examine a problematic situation or action to change it for the better. In PAR projects, the research is not primarily theory development per se and refers more to the practice of collecting and presenting information to inform and mobilize collective action. New theories may emerge from this process, but the emphasis is on generating local knowledge that improves conditions. This can create real tensions for academic researchers who need to navigate meeting the needs of the participants and their own needs to develop ideas that might have application in other contexts. According to Chatterton, Fuller and Routledge (2007), this approach is essentially about knowledge production, whereby knowledge is produced jointly with others, the objective being to produce critical interpretations and readings of the world, which are accessible and understandable to all those involved. In a way, the approach challenges conventional top-down methods of knowledge production. Greenwood, Whyte, and Harkavy (1993) and McIntyre (2008) perceive this approach in a transformative sense, with researchers collaborating fully with communities, learning from them; with a commitment to improve and understand the world beyond academia (see also Stoecker 1999).

In terms of knowledge production, it seeks to generate knowledge through the efforts of the participants themselves, giving them in the process, a greater awareness of their own environment or context. In my view, PAR is about generating knowledge that professionals can share with communities or other groups involved in the process. The word 'participation' is central to this approach, as those involved are known as participants, whatever their level of engagement with the research project. Participation implies different levels of engagement, sometimes describing active involvement in all aspects of a project or limited involvement during particular times. The decision as to who participates, how they participate, when they participate and why they participate exposes real differences amongst researchers and reflects the diversity of PAR projects.

The term "action" in PAR implies that the research encompasses and generates activity and change. However, there are considerable differences in the emphasis given to action in the research including its orientation (e.g. internal or external, personal or collective), scale (local or societal) and frequency (episodic or systemic), all shaped by the context and intentions of the participants. On the other hand, Chatterton, Fuller, and Routledge (2007) argue that the word "action" does not need substitution but re-energizing as too much focus has been placed on research at the expense of action. They assert the need for "putting the activism back into action" and the importance of "academic activists".

However, there are problems in academics taking this activist approach in a country where heritage is highly contested, and for a long time, has also been racialised.

In practice, it seems that researchers often have to deal with different levels of participation as the interest and priorities of the community or communities shift and change, as well as take into account the skills within the community or communities. Greenwood, Whyte, and Harkavy (1993) point to the importance of distinguishing between the participatory intent of the project and the reality. In addition, there is a danger of viewing participation as a single activity, ignoring interactions between the diversity of individual interests, assuming that the group has a clear and consistent identity and that the goals of the project are coherent and uncontested. This is one major criticism this approach might be levelled on in the research area, where the identities of resident communities are multiple, shifting and in a continuous state of flux. There are also a very diverse range of interests, with some communities expecting to improve their general social conditions by promoting heritage as a commercial enterprise. There is an intricate relationship between participation, power and politics within the communities and the effect of the participatory process on external stakeholders (Greenwood, Whyte, and Harkavy 1993; Kindon, Pain and Kesby 2007). This relationship needs further investigation.

In rejecting the possibility of a neutral stance to research, PAR is concerned with the subjectivity of participants, which is a commitment to research that has implications beyond publication in peer-review journals, and an acknowledgement of the relationships between researchers and participants. So, PAR challenges not only the status of researchers as experts but also raises questions about how knowledge is generated.

The view that trained researchers should enter a field with predefined sets of hypotheses that have emerged out of previous research findings, to collect data using 'objective' methods, leave with minimal disruption and not contaminate the site or their results in order to develop theoretical insights, hardly fits with the PAR model. PAR is the ultimate in social science research, with research questions generated by the participants themselves— both of which can change over time. PAR researchers are not dispassionate about those they are working with and often they create strong relationships with people immersed in a process to help change their circumstances. It is through the interactions between participants that true knowledge is generated. The goal is not research for its own sake— it is research focused on making a practical difference to the participants. This means that the actual research methods used can vary significantly with each PAR project.

In conducting this research, I was a participant observer at nearly all levels of the engagement process, from boardroom consultations with descendant communities, capturing their arguments and sentiments about the treatment of human remains by archaeologists, to the reburial of these remains in the landscape, where I witnessed other engagement processes unfolding. While some may perceive this as an administrative requirement, I think researchers must develop another 'ear' in the research process— one that deepens their understanding of communities with whom they engage. This research reflects, to a greater extent, this experience from the viewpoint of the researcher.

3.5 Conclusion: Limitations in the Methodologies

The methods described and discussed in this chapter are in my view adequate for a small project in public or community archaeology. However, there are shortcomings which may arise from some of the methods employed during the research.

With regards to the oral interviews, the shallow depth of the answers obtained led me to reflect whether some of the open-ended questions were effectively responded to by participants. In this context, further discussion outside the structured questionnaire was preferred, but again this was compounded when respondents confessed ignorance to some of the issues raised. This may be criticized as poor data gathering, for which there are a number of ways where valuable information is lost as a result. However, the most important principle in my approach to oral interviews was to align the questionnaire adequately with the research questions. This would elicit the information required to answer the questions.

This research may be criticized on the manner in which I approached archaeological fieldwork, assuming that the sites in question were, or carried, Venda identities in one form or the other and that these identities are archeologically recognizable (Huffman 1996; Huffman and Hanisch 1987). Pre-European historical events of the area are complex since not only the Venda settled in this area, but also other groups as well (Beach 1980 and 1994). Venda links with Mapungubwe are sketchy (Ralushai 2005; Hanisch 2008) and more research is required to document their archaeological identities.

The most prominent debate in southern African Iron Age archeology is the relevance of Venda ethnography in interpreting Mapungubwe as well as Great Zimbabwe type sites (Huffman 1996, 2005 and 2007), as there is an assumption that aspects of contemporary Venda ethnography can be used to account for events dating back to the 13th century. Nineteenth and 20th century ethnographic literature was consulted and used in as much as it informed about community access to cultural heritage resources and how some of these resources are valued in local contexts and tradition. In situations where cultural continuity is demonstrated by archaeological evidence, it is necessary to understand how to use ethnography to interpret the remote past. In this study however, it was not much about interpretation of Mapungubwe and related sites, but about how these sites and landscapes are utilized in the present.

There are various criticisms levelled against PAR, with some scholars arguing that it is not research at all. These scholars view it as consultancy or political activism and disguise the term 'research' to provide its proponents with a cover of legitimacy and credibility that hides the highly subjective nature of its research design. To cope with such criticisms requires researchers with significant tenacity and the ability to navigate the often vastly different worlds in which their research takes place and that of academia. For example, disseminating the findings of a PAR project to a community, may be through websites, drama productions and informal conversations in contrast to peer-reviewed journals, conferences and formally taught courses. The mechanisms to achieve this are not easy, and may sometimes be confused with exercises in public relations.

Like most other social science research, there is no full involvement of the participants in the entire research process. For example, data analysis is often done by the researcher. This may be due to time constraints of the participants, trust in the researcher's skills or recognition that full participation in data analysis can create vulnerability in a group that may be damaging (Cahill 2007).

CHAPTER FOUR
Data Presentation

4.1. Introduction

This chapter presents the data gathered for this research. Starting with archaeological fieldwork, it sets the agenda for cultural heritage conservation as viewed by heritage professionals. The condition assessments detailed here demonstrate conservation and protection from one perspective only. The public perspective is different, if archaeological ethnography is considered. The data presented here also outlines the repatriation and reburial of human remains excavated by researchers from the University of Pretoria and other tertiary institutions in South Africa. Since the dawn of democracy in 1994, individuals and structures representing the descendants of the Mapungubwe people have been requesting government to facilitate the process of repatriation and reburial of all human remains from the Mapungubwe Cultural Landscape (MCL) held by the University of Pretoria. They include the Vhangona Cultural Movement, the Lemba Cultural Association, the San Council, the Tshivhula Royal Family, the Ga-Machete Royal Family and the Leshiba Royal Family. This aspect of the data presented is regarded as 'documenting' tradition—how communities interact and communicate with their pasts in the present, as well as how they perceived conservation of heritage places. The sayings/speeches of role players in the repatriation exercise are also presented in terms of how cultural heritage is politicized and used.

4.2. Archaeological Ethnography

Archeological ethnography as used in this work mainly follows a critique of the "Ethnographic Present" as used by other archaeologists (see Huffman 1996) where direct connections are made on material culture objects made by the Venda speakers with Great Zimbabwe and related stone-walled settlements. Here, references to archaeological ethnography are used in locating the meaning of cultural heritage to descendant communities— whether this heritage is directly connected with those communities or not. Most of this data is gleaned from my participation in the repatriation and reburial of human remains from Mapungubwe during the course of 2006 and 2007, and the oral interviews conducted in Venda during the course of 2008, as a follow-up to the former. The power of this exercise lies in locating the meaning ascribed by descendant communities to certain heritage features, processes, and places. This is largely missing in existing archaeological literature, despite claims to the contrary. As stated in the previous chapter, this project assumes or adopts the premise that the so-called descent or descendant communities are not socio-genealogical or proven genetically linked to the archaeological sites in discussion. The discourse on invented tradition and heritage is simply too complex to be ignored, in view also of the wide ranging discussion on repatriation and intellectual property right of cultural heritage (see Borofsky 1987; Evans 1985; Hughes and Trautmann 1995; Hobsbawm 1983; Hobsbawm and Ranger 1983; Peel 1984).

My approach to archaeological ethnography here is based on the premise that contestations about the past are legitimised through ritual and ceremony (see what Fontein 2006, Ch. 3 refers to as 'connoisseurs of the past'). Focus is on various forms of agency that are indicative of how communication is made with the ancestors, and heritage places. Also important is how the various clans and communities mourn of the loss of tradition following the exhumation of human remains by archaeologists, and how their pasts were stolen. Although the cleansing ceremony prior to the reburial of human remains in the Mapungubwe Cultural Landscape was largely closed to the public, Venda spirit mediums held performances in an effort to appease ancestors of the land. Most of these performances often result in very consistent narratives about the past or the ancestors, regardless of the contestations that may arise. The question is how valuable are these actors in linking scholars to the 'cognitive world' of heritage contests in particular, and the past in general. Mapungubwe's history is largely unknown because of the way the site has been treated by antiquarians and scholars alike. Oral traditions dealing with the post-prehistoric period (for lack of a better term) do not even relate directly to the site. Thus, what we have is not a history, but an archaeological storyline— a storyline which dominates, overshadows, and sidelines other narratives about the site. These alternative narratives are missing or silent. Thus, for the knowledge of Mapungubwe all there is about the past of the place, and local communities are unhappy about this.

4.3. Condition Assessments

Condition surveys or assessments are generally aimed towards capturing site conditions, site size, and threats and potential threats towards their preservation. In archaeology, these are necessary due to the destruction and rapid deterioration of sites, with archaeologists attempting to ascertain the cause and nature of site destruction. This is normally done using a checklist, evaluating site conditions in terms of potential threats, imminent threats or danger and no danger. The objective of the exercise is to capture as many as possible aspects of site degradation. Condition assessments are also an exercise in documentation. This may be achieved through site mapping, recording visible artefacts, features and structures, and through photography. The data is then used for current and future monitoring purposes as well as for making appropriate intervention methods in terms of conservation.

4.3.1 *The stonewalled site on Ratho Farm*

The condition report presented here is summarized from detailed documentation conducted on the site during the field seasons of 2007 and 2008 (Figure 6). The latter survey was done with the assistance and advice of Dr Munyaradzi Manyanga, then a visiting scholar from the University of Zimbabwe, and an expert on the conservation of stonewalled structures of the Zimbabwe Tradition. The detailed notes and photographic record of the site is available for verification and future fieldwork purposes on the site. The exercise was conducted to assess the conservation needs of heritage practitioners on the site and sites of similar nature found in the area (see Huffman and Hanisch 2007).

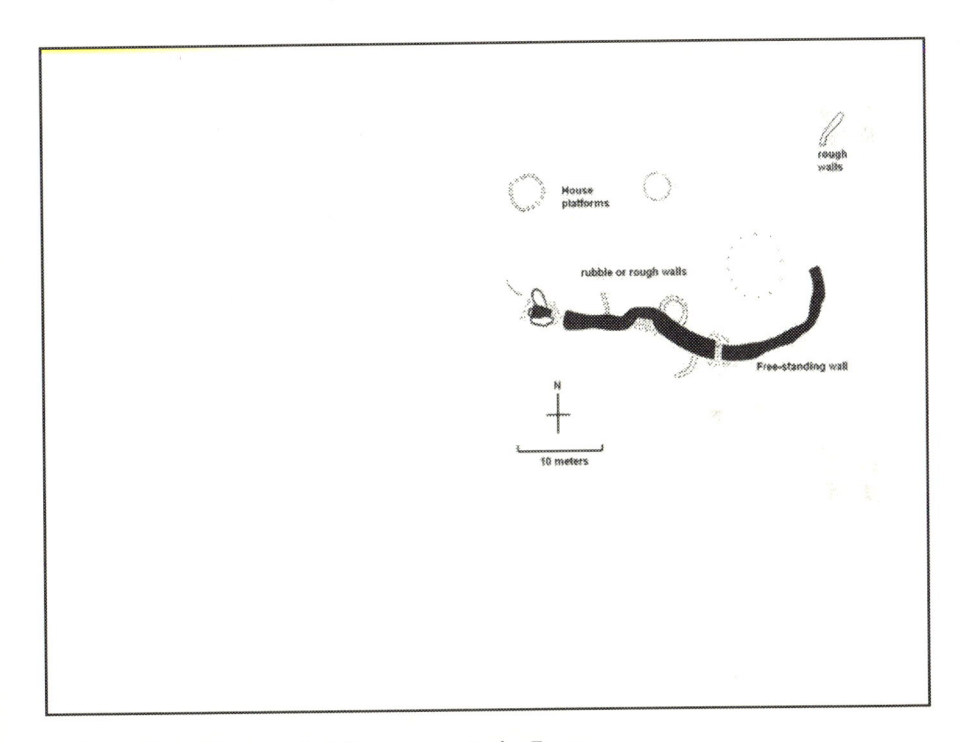

Fig. 6. Plan of Stonewalled Structure on Ratho Farm

SOURCE: Modified from Huffman and Hanisch (1987).

The presentation in Figure 7 displays a bulge on left and right of the wall (Figure 7). There is a displacement of stone slabs and evidence of toppling. This suggests structural weakness. The coursing shows use of wedges to maintain consistent levels. This is eventually giving in due to weight of the stone slabs. The stabilization of the core is required to conserve the walls.

Fig. 7. Bulging Wall Face at Ratho (Photo by the Author)

Fig. 8. The General Wall Appearance of the South-eastern Sections of the Stonewalled
Structure at Ratho (Photo by the Author).

Several sections of the wall display bulging and the wall is sinking (see
Figure 8) due to the foundation and the instability of the core material.

Fig. 9. Deteriorating Rock Slabs; South Wall Sections, Ratho (Photo by the Author)

Rock slabs are deteriorating. There is splitting and walls separating, members becoming loose and falling down (Figure 9).

The wall collapse is creating room for movement of stone slabs. The entire foundation may be the cause of the problem. There is, however, a stability factor in that the walls are mostly resting on rock outcrop, but there are sections where these walls are based on earth/gravel. The collapse is covering a wall underneath as sections of wall faces are visible, and to further ascertain this, what is required is to remove it systematically.

Fig. 10. Rough Walling to South, Stretching Westwards, Ratho (Photo by Author)

Figure 10 displays little or no coursing and was a later addition to the neatly coursed free standing walls mentioned above. The purpose of this additional walling is not immediately clear as we have no excavations to assist with site chronology and development. The structural problems of this wall are difficult to define because coursing is irregular or non-existent.

Assessing Structural Problems at Ratho Zimbabwe

The bulging that was recorded on several wall sections is probably a result of an unstable core or foundation, the latter of which is both earth and rock. The horizontal or vertical separation of rocks— splitting or shearing—is a result of poor bonding or the coursing. Toppling, which is the displacement of stones from the top courses, is a result of wild animals, especially baboons and monkeys, hunting for scorpions and insects. Vegetation is also a factor, where you find trees falling on the wall sides and the top (Figure 11).

Fig. 11. The Effects of Vegetation on the Stonewalled Structure at Ratho

(Photo by the Author).

Progressive collapse is evident in a number of places, and this creates instability in the structures—triggering further, subsequent and more severe collapses (Figure 12).

Fig. 12. A Severe Collapse Caused by Bulging and Perhaps Instability of the Core as well as Wall Foundation (Photo by the Author).

The site condition at Ratho stonewalled structure may be evaluated as follows: The site is generally in a fair condition, as the structure is stable. However, some immediate action is necessary to stall progressive collapses identified in a number of areas, as this may create an unstable structure in the future. The effect of vegetation is minimal, save for a few places where trees interfere with the structures and features, and where damage is quite significant, leading to rubble. Here damage is near-severe. Toppling is a serious problem as the area roams with baboons. This has resulted in numerous stone blocks falling on the foot of the standing walls (see summary in Table 1).

Table 1. Assessing the causes and severity of structural problems at Ratho

Structural problem	1	2	3	4	5
Settling		X			
Bulging			X		
Splitting			X		
Toppling			X		
Progressive collapse			X		
Activities of wild animals	X				
Burrowing animals	X				
Vegetation encroachment	X		X		
Tree and bush growth		X			
Visitors	X				
Vandalism					
Other	X				

Key to assessing levels of severity
1. minimal or superficial damage
2. significant damage
3. severe damage
4. complete damage
5. site completely removed

The conservation of this particular site requires both an architect and an archaeologist. The architect will face challenges connected with the largely uncoursed stone wall which is definitely a later addition (see Figures 6, 10 and 13).

Fig. 13. Some Rough or Rubble Wall Sections at Ratho (Photo by the Author).

Architecture defines problems on the basis of regularity/patterns. Wild animals, particularly baboons, are a problem, as these are abetting the structural problems of the various structures.

4.3.2 Bambandyanalo (K2)

This site is located just south-east of the Shashe-Limpopo confluence, about a kilometre south-west of Mapungubwe Hill (Figure 5). It is in some kind of amphitheatre, surrounded by sandstone hills (Figure 14).

It is mostly accessed from the south and east. It is an extensive later Iron Age site (AD 1000–1220), covering at least 5 hectares (Meyer 1998) with cultural deposits attributed to the Leopard's Kopje tradition (Huffman 1996, 2005, and 2007). The deposits consist of a homestead, livestock pens and middens (domestic waste heaps). The settlement pattern appears to be characterized by a homestead, located in the centre and now represented by cattle dung deposits, surrounded by homesteads located closer to the sandstone hills and entrances to the valley. For a detailed description of visible features and photographs of the site, the reader is referred to Meyer (1998), who conducted the most extensive excavations on the site. My work concentrated on the central midden, which overlies the cattle dung deposits. These deposits were excavated in 1935 by Gardner (1963), the marks of which are still visible today as the site was not properly backfilled. The excavations directed by J. F. Eloff and A. Meyer during the periods 1968–1970, 1971–1984, 1992–1995, and 1996–2000 within the framework of the Greefswald Archaeology Project further extended earlier excavations and the build up of archaeological material and human skeletal remains kept at the University of Pretoria, mostly in the Anatomy Department. The site was rehabilitated by SANParks as a project in poverty alleviation for the communities from nearby municipal areas (Nienaber and Hutten 2006).

Fig. 14. An Aerial View of the Site of Bambandyanalo in the Foreground, Mapungubwe Hill is the Middle Ground, and the Limpopo River in the Background

(Courtesy of Mapungubwe Museum, University of Pretoria).

The site presented a different set of conservation problems and needs. A condition survey of the kind conducted on the stonewalled structure at Ratho was not possible here. Instead, a comparative documentation of the state of archaeological deposits from the first excavations to the current rehabilitation of the material was done. Figure 15 is a map or plan of the site of Bambandyanalo showing a history of the excavations conducted since 1934 (see Meyer 1998, 61).

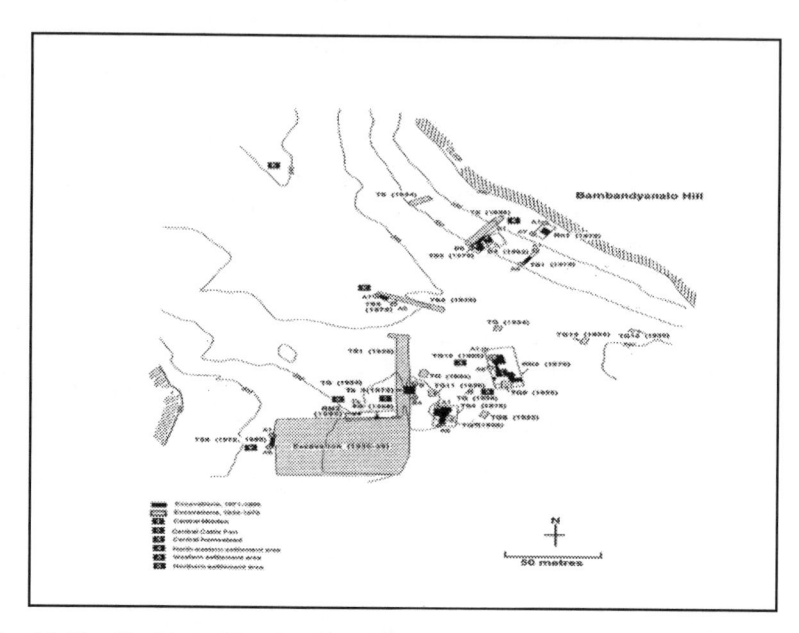

Fig. 15. The Site Plan of Bambandyanalo

    SOURCE: Modified from Meyer 1998.

Figure 16 is an aerial view of the site in 1972 (Meyer 1998, 13) and Figure 17 shows the current state of conservation/presentation at the site, especially the central midden.

Fig. 16. Aerial View of the Site of K2 Showing the 'Scars' of Past Archaeological Excavations (Photo courtesy of Mapungubwe Museum, University of Pretoria).

The site is subjected to soil erosion and the effects of wild animals, especially elephants that stampede on the ash deposits.

Fig. 17. The Current State of Preservation and Presentation of the Central Midden Deposits at K2 (Photo courtesy of Johan Nel)

4.4. Repatriation and Reburial of Human Remains from the Mapungubwe Cultural Landscape

The Mapungubwe Cultural Landscape (MCL) is home to the first civilization or ancient chiefdom and state society in southern Africa. Situated around the Shashe-Limpopo confluence, it covers an extensive region, which is now a region geographically shared by South Africa, Botswana and Zimbabwe. From 900 to 1000 AD, farming societies were operating in the region—hunting wild animals, mostly elephants. A chiefdom based at Bambandyanalo (K2) between 1000 and 1200 AD exploited the Limpopo flood plain quite intensively as well as traded with the western Indian Ocean zone. From 1220 AD, Mapungubwe Hill (Figure 18) was settled, and developed into the capital of a kingdom with extensive regional and continental networks of trade and interaction. Archaeological evidence attests to the existence of a palace complex and a cemetery on the hilltop where royals were buried with gold and other objects. The kingdom ceased to flourish around AD 1300 (Huffman 2007).

Fig. 18. A view of Mapungubwe Hill from the North, Showing the Vertical Cliff Face and a Partial View of Archaeological Deposits on the Summit

(Photo taken by Author).

Traditions and stories of a hill where people were buried in gold have attracted treasure hunters to this region of the Limpopo valley. Following a lead from these stories, a European family re-discovered the site with the "cooperation" of a local resident, Mowena, during the early 1930s, and systematic pillage of the artefacts and the integrity of the archaeological deposits began. The site was subsequently reported to the University of Pretoria, which began a programme of archaeological research in 1933. Most of the human remains excavated by archaeologists, have, until their repatriation, been housed in the university's Department of Anatomy. Other South African research institutions such as the University of the Witwatersrand and the National Cultural History Museum subsequently became involved and collected some material as well as human remains from the site as well as adjacent Bambandyanalo (K2) and other sites in the surrounding landscape. By the time the remains were repatriated in 2007, some 143 human remains were claimed by descendant communities (Nienaber *et al.* 2008).

The process and procedures of the repatriation are described in detail in Nienaber *et al.* (2008). The repatriation of the Mapungubwe remains came at a time when some scholars were of the view that human remains should be returned to the communities where they came from originally as part of the national healing process (Legassic and Rasool 2000). Presented here are details regarding the repatriation process, the communities involved, and the ceremonies conducted. There has been some discussion in South Africa in terms of approaches to repatriation and how potential conflicts with descendant communities could be handled (Steyn and Nienaber 2005).

4.4.1 *Negotiations*

The process of repatriation began when a request was made to the then President of South Africa, Thabo Mbeki, by the Khoka Foundation on behalf of representatives of the descendants of Mapungubwe. These representatives included the Lemba Cultural Association, Machete Royal Family, Tshivhula Royal Council, Vhangona Cultural Movement and the San Council. This resulted in negotiations between the parties involved, as well as within the various university committees, government departments and heritage agencies (Figure 19). Representatives of the Machete, Tshivhula, and Vhangona clans regarded themselves as Vhatwamamba, or 'original inhabitants of Vhutwamamba', the land to the north-western part of the Soutpansberg mountains. This 'indigenous' status is designed to underline the layered nature of Venda origins, where some clans, collectively known as Vhangona (Vhadau, Vhakwevo, Vhamfamadi, Vhania, Vhangoni, Vhalea and Vhaluvhu) are regarded (largely uncontested) as the original inhabitants of Venda. However, there are some groups such as the Machete and Leshiba royal families, who do not appear in the early ethnographic records (see Earle *et al.* 2006; Loubser 1988 and 1992), and might be an example of an 'invented community' for the sake of heritage ownership. The Machete, Leshiba and Tshivhula claim to have been re-located from the Mapungubwe area, and are currently involved in land claims around Mapungubwe. Some Vhangona claim that Mapungubwe was their capital.

The negotiations were done in accordance with the requirements of the South African Heritage Resources Act which ensures consultation on new projects and facilitates the repatriation of human remains (see details in Nienaber *et al.* 2008). The negotiations were long, difficult, emotional, and nearly collapsed at one stage as claimant communities disagreed on procedure, distrusted one another and lost confidence in the facilitator, who happened to be the Deputy Minister of Environmental Affairs and Tourism, and thus a very senior government official. In summary, within the framework of the Mapungubwe Steering Committee, shared responsibility, co-operation and trust among the parties involved made it possible for the research institutions to release human remains to their owners without objections. The University of Pretoria, the National Cultural History Museum (now Ditsong National Museum of Cultural History) and the University of Witwatersrand demonstrated considerable readiness and willingness to accept claims for human remains to be repatriated and reburied at their places of origin. This acceptance changed the complexion of archaeological practice in South Africa, where archaeological collections and associated human remains were linked with living, indigenous, descendant communities and recognized as the remains of their ancestors.

Fig. 19. Negotiations for the Reburial of the Human Remains with Communities from Venda (Photo by the Author).

As a member of the University of Pretoria Mapungubwe Committee, I was involved in all the meetings. However, on ethical grounds, I am not able to provide details of the proceedings of some of the meetings, in view of the difficulty of the negotiation processes, the emotions exuded by negotiating parties and individuals, and the conflicts which arose, but fortunately resolved during the process. In the end, all were committed to what could be done and achieved, hence the successful outcome of the negotiations. It should be added at this stage that even the subsequent stages of the process were also (re)negotiated to the satisfaction of communities, or at least, compromise decisions were reached in view of the cultural diversity of the communities involved, local traditions, etc (see Schoeman and Pikirayi 2011).

4.4.2 *The Symbolic Handover Ceremony*

A total of 143 human remains, originally buried in the MCL, were handed over to representatives of descendants from this area at a well attended ceremony held at the University of Pretoria on 29 October 2007. I was a participant observer at this ceremony, which was also attended by representatives of heritage agencies and local municipal authorities. The South African government was represented by the Deputy Minister of Environmental Affairs and Tourism, Mrs. Rejoice Mabudafhasi, whose department facilitated the protracted negotiations between communities and institutions. She described the ceremony as something more than just returning the dead to the MCL: "...this symbolic handover ceremony is not just about signalling to return the dead to the Mapungubwe Cultural Landscape. It is also about recognising the importance of local custodians and beliefs, and confirms that the community voices have been heard".

She also remarked that by accepting the claims for human remains, the institutions that had been keeping these remains have shown commitment towards the common goal of addressing the injustices of South Africa's shared past whilst promoting healing within communities and reconciliation between previously conflicting parties.

Communities received the human remains with considerable ululation and jubilations. Mr Khosi Maisa, speaking on behalf of the Mapungubwe Steering Committee Chairperson, Khosi Ramovha, remarked that it was their duty to request their ancestors be treated with respect through the repatriation and reburial of their remains: "This is in accordance with our belief that once our people are buried, they should not be disturbed. Our acceptance of our ancestors' remains back to where they belong is emotionally gratifying and an awesome experience.... This is the homecoming reunion and an important healing process for our communities".

The Director of the National Cultural History Museum, Mr Makgolo Makgolo, unequivocably apologised for the manner in which research institutions have continued to retain human remains in their collections for purposes of research and display. Professor Calie Pistorius, the then University of Pretoria Vice-Chancellor and Principal, briefly explained the circumstances leading to the human remains being part of the history of the University of Pretoria, but more important, also apologised for what has happened.

4.4.3 *The Cleansing Ceremony*

This cleansing was traditional protocol for healing in preparation for the reburial of Mapungubwe human remains (Figures 20 and 21). The Department of Environmental Affairs and Tourism, in collaboration with

The Freedom Park Trust and the Department of Sports, Arts and Culture in Limpopo, hosted a Cleansing and Healing Ceremony as well as the return of the spirits in the Mapungubwe National Park. Starting with sacred ceremonies on 5 November 2007, traditional activities were concluded with a cleansing and healing ceremony including the return of the spirits to the site of Mapungubwe on 6 November 2007. I attended the official ceremony representing the University of Pretoria and presented a speech.

Fig. 20. Some of the Traditional Leaders Who Graced the Cleansing Ceremony (Photo by the Author)

The ceremony was well-attended by Government officials, heritage professional, claimant communities and their representatives, as well as other interested and invited groups. The Deputy Minister of Environmental Affairs and Tourism, Mrs Rejoice Mabudafhasi was again given an opportunity to speak at this event, which she described as:

> ...a dignified return of the spirits of the Mapungubwe ancestors to their home where they will rest in peace. This is a very public acknowledgement of the moral case for the return of the remains and spirits of the Mapungubwe ancestors thus honouring the traditions of communities and demonstrating the generosity of spirit that this process required of all of us.

Mongane Wally Serote, Chief Executive Officer of The Freedom Park Trust, said repatriation and reburial are organically linked to cleansing, healing and return of the spirits. His organisation has initiated a number of cleansing and healing ceremonies, nationally as well as in Botswana, Swaziland, Mozambique, Tanzania, the United States of America and Namibia, to assist South Africa in the process of forgiveness, reconciliation and moving forward as a truly multiracial society. Mr Wally Serote stated that throughout the world it was common practice that when people die, they are normally buried at home or somewhere that the family members have access to:

> Where individuals die on battlefields or where it is impossible to physically bring remains home, Africans traditionally bring them back home, so that they are integrated with a pool of ancestors who will look after the living. Failure to bring these spirits home renders it impossible for the particular families to integrate their loved ones with their ancestors and thus prevents a sense of closure in that family.

> Cleansing and healing cuts across beliefs, traditions, customs and culture in the African continent. As such, the ceremony will allow different groups to perform rituals according to their belief systems. A space will also be identified for descendents to intercede once the ceremonies have been concluded.

In her keynote address, the Member of the Executive Council (MEC) for Sports, Arts and Culture in Limpopo, Mrs Joyce Mashamba remarked that "this cleansing ceremony once again confirms the role of traditional healers and elderly people as mediators between communities and their ancestors...."

Fig. 21. Part of the Crowd that Attended the Cleansing Ceremony and the Official
    Ceremony to Mark the Occasion (Photo by the Author).

4.4.4 *The Reburial Ceremony*

Reburial ceremonies took place from the 18th to the 20th of November
2007. The human remains were re-buried in carefully prepared shafts at
the sites of Schroda, an Iron Age farming community site dating AD 900–
1000; Hamilton, Mapungubwe Hill, Bambandyanalo and near the new
interpretation centre. The process was supervised by SANParks and
archaeologists from the University of Pretoria as well as representatives
from the Department of Environmental Affairs and Tourism (DEAT),
South African Heritage Resources Agency (SAHRA), and invited
provincial and municipal authorities.

The University of Pretoria, through the Archaic Heritage Project
Management, together with the Department of Anatomy, was involved in
the repatriation of the human remains. The process entailed preparation of
suitable coffins for the human remains, their conservation and interim
curation according to accepted international standards, and the
transportation and final reburial of the remains (Nienaber *et al.* 2008). A
graphic documentation of the events is given in Figures 22–24.

Fig. 22. Accompanying Their Ancestors to Their Final Resting Place— Venda and Other Communities in the Reburial Ceremony at Mapungubwe (Photo courtesy of Johan Nel).

Traditional leaders and representatives from the Venda clans/communities were given an opportunity to speak about their views of the reburial and cleansing ceremonies. The President of the Vhangona Cultural Movement, Mr Sigwavhulimu said Mapungubwe was now the "New Mecca", implying that it had acquired its spiritual importance and was worth making a cultural 'pilgrimage' to. Silas Sebola of the Tshivhula Royal Family who regard themselves as custodians of the vaTwanamba (original inhabitants of the area around Mapungubwe) said that the ceremony was important so that communities ask for forgiveness from ancestral spirits. He perceived a process of restoring the value and dignity of Mapungubwe, as well as speeding up land restitution since some of the Venda clans have laid claims on surrounding farms. Petros Machete of the Machete Royal Family, which has made land claims near Mapungubwe, noted that there are Venda-specific ways of performing their ceremonies and rituals, which must be properly followed. Calvin Leshiba, Chairperson of the Leshiba Royal Family, commented that the reburial signified the return of the spirits of their ancestors to their original land (see, Figures 23 and 24). The President of the Lemba Cultural Association saw reburial as an opportunity to integrate with other communities.

Fig. 23. Finalizing the Reburial of Human Remains at K2. Note the Central Midden to the Left Where the Remains Were Excavated (Photo courtesy of Johan Nel).

Other representatives such as Mrs. Joyce Mashamba noted that the ceremony symbolically brought the ancestors back home, which the people welcomed. This stressed the need to preserve the associated cultural heritage. Her comments fall in line with a quotation from Andre Gide, French critic, essayist, and novelist (1869– 1951): "So long as we live...let us cherish humanity". One can read from this statement that the conservation of cultural heritage in the Mapungubwe Cultural Landscape was meaningless before the reburial and cleansing ceremonies. This also has implications on tradition and community perceptions on conservation. The analysis and interpretation of the data is the subject of chapters 5 and 6.

Individuals and communities or clans representing the descendants of the Mapungubwe people eventually received records of the reburial process of the remains of their ancestors from the DEAT at a function that was held at Mapungubwe National Park.

Fig. 24. The Communities Accompanied the Reburial with Ritual and Ceremony (Photo, courtesy of Johan Nel).

4.5. Oral Interviews

A total of 66 responses were solicited from informants from various clans and a wide range of age groups (see Tables 2 and 3).

Table 2. Informants grouped by clan identity

Clan name or identity	Number of respondents	Frequency (%)
Lemba	24	33.36
Masenzi	1	1.52
Mushavhi	3	4.55
Singo	1	1.52
Tshivhula	3	4.55
Vhalea	1	1.52
Vhangona	29	43.94
Vhavenda	1	1.52
Identity not revealed	3	4.55
Total	66	100.00

Table 3. Informants categorised according to age groups

Age group	Number of informants	Frequency (%)
< or = 20	7	10.61
21–30	43	65.15
31–40	6	9.09
41–50	2	3.03
> 50	7	10.61
Age of informant not revealed	1	1.52
Total	**66**	**100.00**

The participants in Venda were presented with a questionnaire to respond to statements, initially in writing, to gauge their thoughts and suggestions on the subject of cultural heritage conservation in the Limpopo Province and the repatriation to and reburial of human remains in the Mapungubwe Cultural Landscape. Where participates were not able or were unwilling to write their responses on the questionnaire, they were at liberty to express themselves orally, and more important, in the vernacular. This became the preferred approach instead of leaving the questionnaire to be completed by the participants. The latter option always resulted in sketchy or poor answers, mostly hurried and thus compromising the integrity of the data collection exercise. To further assist in the process, I engaged a field assistant knowledgeable not only in the TshiVenda language, but also on the local clan dynamics and politics. The resultant oral enquiry could then be modified to tally the process of data gathering. The data presented here is compiled from the responses of the candidates to the questions posed to them. The informants are cited here together with their age to give an idea of the structure of the population, the nature of responses from the various age groups, as well as their concerns in matters of cultural heritage.

4.5.1 *Awareness of Cultural Heritage Conservation Programmes*

A majority of the informants (61) were aware of conservation programmes on archaeological sites, while only 5 were unaware. Nine (9) informants pointed out that they have been involved in the conservation programmes in one way or the other, while 57 were not or have never been involved. Some only become aware of these through the electronic and print media (Ramudzuli Ludwig Muhadi, 28; Ludhere Fulufhelo, 19). This awareness was sometimes enhanced by the fact that some of these informants were already working as tour guides or security guards in cultural heritage sites in Venda such as the stonewalled site of Dzata (Fredy Vele, 25; Lucy Marubini, 27, Rudzani Mavhungu, 26; Gladys Malindi Atshilovha, 35).

4.5.2 *Informants' Views on the Conservation Programmes*

This question elicited a wide range of responses, from very poorly thought standard answers to well thought out ones. Responses such as "I think they are ok" (*sic*) or "Archaeologists are doing a great job!" were rejected as they failed to provide adequate answers to the question.

Mr Hamisi (aged 77) from Makhado complained that the conservation programmes are done without consulting the communities. Mr Thobakgale (77) was content that conservation preserves heritage. Compared to the 1930s when they excavated human remains without permission from local, descendant communities, current conservation is quite acceptable (Govan Mabirimisa, 26). One informant even indicated in his response that these conservation programmes saved Thulamela from "total collapse" (Kudzani Mulaudzi, 29). Current conservation programmes are helping the young understand their origins and cultural heritage (Thiathu Nicholus Madzhie, 30). There should be educational programmes so that communities know their roles regarding nearby archaeological sites. It is through such programmes that communities will participate in cultural heritage conservation (Ramudzuli Ludwig Muhadi, 28). Other informants thought current conservation programmes will promote tourism and increase visitor numbers in the province (Munyadziwa Hulisani, 21; Lucy Marubini, 27). One informant said we need archaeologists to assist in descendant communities' claims for ownership of archaeological sites such as Mapungubwe (Roshuma Luvhengo, 22).

Other informants wanted to see the involvement of local people or elders (Gladys Malindi Atshilovha, 35; Munzhedzi Vele (*age not given*); Mufunwa Mulaudzi, 28; Ludere Fulufhelo, 19; Radzilani Mulatedzi 23), as these programmes must be community-based, and should not be run by government, mining companies and non-governmental organisations (Godfrey Nephawe, 58), as is currently the case. One informant suggested a desk within the Venda Traditional Council to facilitate the conservation of cultural heritage (Ramudzuli Ludwig Muhadi, 28). While others were generally satisfied with current cultural conservation programmes in the province, they pointed out that these needed further development, with much work to be done (Muvhango Pfuluwani, 27; Lovey Tshivhula 26, Mavis Naledzani, 30; Muswuni Hulisani, 26; Fulufhelo Madumela, 30; Mufunwa Mulaudzi, 28). Some conservation programmes appear to be not well-planned (Naledzani Thompho, 22). Some suggested that archaeologists must increase their awareness programmes so that communities understand what they are trying to do and hopefully get involved (Fanie Marunzhe, 27). Others pointed out that conservation must not only focus on well-known heritage sites, but also on less developed sites such as the Dalavhuredzi Footprint site (Mutshekwa Ndwamato, 26).

Another major concern with current cultural heritage conservation programmes seems to be the "free*zing* of heritage" (*own emphasis*) to make it belong just to the past, instead of creating a living one relevant to the present (Kenneth Sadiku, 29).

4.5.3 *Level of Involvement in Cultural Heritage Conservation*

In this section, I treat awareness and direct involvement as different realms. A few informants were directly and already involved in cultural heritage conservation as tour guides at Dzata (Fredy Vele, 25, Rudzani Mavhungu, aged 26). Some have been involved with the reconstruction of Dzata stone walls (Gladys Malindi Atshilovha, 35), and one was involved in the conservation of Dalavhuredzi Footprint site, and represented the community of Mufulwi. Some university students have been involved in the excavation of some stonewalled sites associated with the Ngona at Mugobi Hill and the University of Pretoria project on narratives of Mapungubwe by the Drama Department (Godfrey Nephawe, 58). One informant was a claimant of human remains from Mapungubwe, representing the Tshivhula Royal Family (Lovey Tshivhula, 26); another works in the Department of Arts and Culture (Raymond Ramabulana, 30). Some of these informants wanted to assume more responsibilities in cultural heritage conservation (Gladys Malindi Atshilovha, 35; Muhadi Masala, 38; Ravele Pfuluwani, 30).

It can be surmised from this that the level of cultural heritage awareness, interest and involvement is *not insignificant* among the various Venda communities or clans, especially the younger age groups (21–30 years). It would be interesting to find, in a future study, how this knowledge is imparted to them at such an early stage.

4.5.4 *How Informants Want to Be Involved in Site Conservation*

This question was targeted to informants not currently involved in cultural heritage conservation but instead those who were aware of what were happening in their areas in particular and province in general. Again, the responses were variable, but nonetheless, interesting.

At the age of 77, Thobakgale from Makhado still felt that if given an assignment, he would still be able to do what he has the capacity to do. However, the relatively younger Senoamadi (70) confessed that he was too old to be involved. The younger generation had a wider range of responses. Some did not want to be involved, preferring that archaeologists and heritage managers do the work (Rendani Muletshothe, 23). Others wanted to be involved as local community members or representatives in consultation with cultural heritage authorities (Roshuma Luvhengo, 22; Dephney Muselankoe, 25; Mufungwa Mulaudzi, 28). Others preferred 'stakeholder' involvement in the management of these sites (Fanie Marunzhe, 27), or teaching their own community about "cultural development" (Rendani Vhuhwavho, 24). Some simply wanted to help generate knowledge about the past (Shumani Manenzhe, 21; Frank Khwandu, 50). Others wanted to be part of any development project affecting heritage sites (Tshililo Khakhu, 40; Govan Mabirimisa, 26) in their local traditional councils (Mutshekwa Tshilidzi, 27). One informant was keen to develop a local site (Nicolus Manzhie, 24). Other informants wanted to market sites to tourists (Tendani Ramulongo, 25; Tshitaudzi Pfunzo, 29)— transporting people to heritage places (Mothudi Shumani, 22); or just being part of decision-making (Muvhango Pfuluwani, Percy Ramuhashi, 23; Lovey Tshivhula , 26; Mavis Naledzani, 30; Fulufhelo Madumela, 30), or generally conserving Venda heritage (Kenneth Sadiku, 29, Mashige Takalani, 46, Elisa Mammbona 39; Rendani Gangashe 24). Two informants wanted to be involved but had no idea how this could be done (Phathutshedzo Munyadziwa, 17; Jeniffer Mukwevho, 21). Perhaps the age factor counts here, to some extent.

In the current socio-political environment where securing employment is difficult, some informants indicated they wanted to be given internships (Masala Mulalo, 25; Rofhiwa Munyadziwa, 23; Thabelo Muofhe, 19). Others wanted to secure jobs in the field of cultural heritage conservation (Alice Ramulongo, 19; Radzilani Mukovhe, 26; Naledzani Masala, 27, Humbulani Siwadawada 32, Mulaudzi Ndivhuwo, 23; Emmanuel Sing, 26; Ndlovu Tsiluvhu Evelyn, 41; Muswuni Hulisani, 26, Naledzani Thompho, 22; Mavhunga Pelwebe 19; Kudzani Mulaudzi, 29; Radzilani Mulatedzi 23).

4.5.5 *Traditional Methods for Conserving Heritage Places*

The responses received were to a large extent vague, but some indicated that they did not know any methods connected with cultural heritage conservation (Mufungwa Mulaudzi, 28). Some saw nothing wrong with western approaches to cultural heritage conservation as long as they incorporated local beliefs and customs (Roshuma Luvhengo, 22). Some suggested the involvement of traditional, community leaders and older people since these knew more about cultural heritage and sacred places (Ramudzuli Ludwig Muhadi, Lucy Marubini, Rudzani Mavhungu, aged 26, Nicolus Manzhie, 24, Percy Ramuhashi, 23; Ndlovu Tsiluvhu Evelyn 41, Govan Mabirimisa, 26; Naledzani Alidzuli, 70). Entry into some of these sites requires the permission of the local traditional leadership who must organise a ceremony (Thiathu Nicholus Madzhie, 30), e.g. *Miphaso* (a ceremony that connects the living with ancestors) (Naledzani Takalani, 25, Rudzani Mavhungu, aged, 26). In conserving sites, customs of a particular place should be encouraged (Naledzani Masala, 27; Muhadi Masala, 38; Muswuni Hulisani, 26), and archaeologists must respect local traditions and beliefs (Rendani Mambona, 19; Jeniffer Mukwevho, 21; Lovey Tshivhula, 26; Tshililo Khakhu, 40; Ravele Pfuluwani, 30, Govan Mabirimisa, 26). Local descendant communities are the custodians of local heritage and archaeologists must consult them (Radzilani Mulatedzi, 23). These customs must be spelt out by local chiefs and their advisors (Naledzani Alidzuli, 70; Ndlovu Tsiluvhu Evelyn 41, Mutshekwa Tshilidzi, 27; Thabelo Muofhe, 19; George Mudau 36; Rendani Muletshothe, 23). Any attempt to "freeze" cultural heritage as is happening in current conservation practices (Kenneth Sadiku, 29) destroys the inner connections that communities have with archaeological sites.

Sacred sites need protection and care (Tendani Ramulongo, 25; Elisa Mammbona, 39; Raymond Ramabulana, 30; Fulufhelo Madumela, 30; Rendani Vhuhwavho, 24) and archaeologists must consider engaging locals (Mavis Naledzani, 30; Ludhere Fulufhelo, 19; Shumani Manenzhe, 21) and using local resources in conservation (Mavhunga Pelwebe, 19). Elders must be consulted in any communication and participation in development or conservation programmes (Masala Mulalo, 25; Rofhiwa Munyadziwa, 23; Mutshekwa Ndwamato, 26). Cleansing ceremonies are a way of speaking to ancestors (Mutshekwa Ndwamato, 26) and these should be conducted at some heritage places.

More radical views suggested non- or minimal interference with cultural heritage sites. Minimal human intervention is recommended since these sites and areas have remained intact for a very long time without the prescription of conservationists and cultural heritage practitioners. Human beings will always only impact on these places negatively despite efforts to protect them (Ramavhule Mukhode, 27).

Rituals and ceremonies aside, other informants suggested the use of local people and knowledge because such people are the custodian of everything "traditional" and have a better knowledge than the so-called 'experts' (Munzhedzi Vele [*age not given*]; Kudzani Mulaudzi, 29). 'Experts' are advised not to fence off sites or exclude locals from their conservation as locals are also owners of such places (Naledzani Thompho, 22).

4.5.6 Traditional Ceremonies Archaeologists May Consider in Conserving Sites

Cleansing ceremonies must be performed annually or frequently to protect sites from evil spirits (Tshitaudzi Pfunzo, 29) and appease the spirits that live in them (Fanie Marunzhe, 27). In any reburial ceremony, humans must be accompanied by goods such as spears, hoes, knives, pots and beads (Raulinga Hamisi, 77). Some informants pointed out that there are no specific ceremonies required (Frank Khwandu, 50; Thobakgale, 70), while others said there are no such ceremonies (Ramudzuli Ludwig Muhadi, 28; Foche Mudzunga, 20). Only correct rituals are necessary (Senoamadi, 70) as long as their performance does not distort history or the past of these places (Thobakgale, 70). One informant said the brewing of beer would appease the spirits residing in these sites. This would also maintain the value of these places as well as the respect they deserve (Munzhedzi Vele, *age not supplied*).

Some informants wanted to see the re-introduction of circumcision schools (Phathutshedzo Munyadziwa, aged 17) as well as the performance of ritual and cleansing ceremonies in places considered sacred such as river valleys and mountains (Godfrey Nephawe, 58). The majority mentioned the *Domba* (a pre-marital initiation ceremony) (22), *Tshikona* (a male dance where each player has a pipe made from special local bamboo only grown in Thohoyandou and Sibasa areas) (22), *Musevhetho* (a ceremony for young girls) (20), and, *Murundu* or *Mula* (main initiation for boys) (18) ceremonies as critical in conservation, but did not explain how these would help the protection of archaeological heritage. Other ceremonies mentioned are *Tshifasi* (a dance performed by young, not yet married girls) (6 respondents), *Tshikombela* or *Tshigombela* (a dance usually performed by married women) (4 respondents), *Vusha or Vhukomba* (a ceremony for girls who have just reached puberty) (2 respondents), *Tshilani* (2 respondents), rainmaking (3 respondents), and cleansing (4 respondents). Eleven respondents indicated that they did not know which ceremonies were important for cultural heritage conservation.

4.5.7 Views on the Importance of the Mapungubwe Reburial Ceremonies

A variety of interesting responses was made. Only qualitative answers were considered here. Answers such as "It was a good thing" were rejected as they did not provide sufficient explanation on the importance of such an event.

Rendani Muletshothe (23) who attended the re-burial events at Mapubungubwe, described it as a touching, emotional event. Some informants saw it as a blessing and pleasing to their ancestral spirits (Hamisi, Masala Mulalo, 25; Dasie Mphephu Takalani Andries 63). The reburial ceremonies brought an awareness of their past (Thobakgale, 70). Most saw it as an important thing to happen as their ancestors 'were brought back home' (Senoamadi, Munyadziwa Hulisani, 21; Fredy Vele, 25, Naledzani Takalani, 25, Foche Mudzunga, 20, Radzilani Mukovhe, 26, Jeniffer Mukwevho, 21, Percy Ramuhashi, 23, Kenneth Sadiku, 29; Mavis Naledzani 30; Tshitaudzi Pfunzo, 29; Singo Thilivhali 30, Mulaudzi Ndivhuwo, 23, Elisa Mammbona, 39) and 'finally laid to rest' (Nicolus Manzhie, 24; Mutshekwa Ndwamato, 26; Muhadi Masala, 38, Muswuni Hulisani, 26; Dephney Muselankoe, 25, Roshuma Luvhengo, 22; Govan Mabirimisa, 26; Mufungwa Mulaudzi, 28). The ancestors were now resting in peace, in a place where they belong (Tendani Ramulongo, 25; Muhadi Masala, 38), and the community was now at peace with the past (Godfrey Nephawe, 58; Tshililo Khakhu, 40; Dasie Mphephu Takalani Andries 63, Ndlovu Tsiluvhu Evelyn, 41; Rofhiwa Munyadziwa, 23; Raymond Ramabulana, 30; Muswuni Hulisani, 26; Rendani Muletshothe, 23; Roshuma Luvhengo, 22; Fulufhelo Madumela, 30; Rendani Vhuhwavho, 24; Mavhunga Pelwebe, 19; Shumani Manenzhe, 21; Lovey Tshivhula 26).

The ceremonies were also about respect and honour bestowed to the dead (Fanie Marunzhe, 27; Kudzani Mulaudzi, 29, Radzilani Mulatedzi, 23; Rudzani Mavhungu, 26) and respect to humanity (Munzhedzi Vele, *age not supplied*) and their ancestors, from where communities got their 'blessings'. It rained soon after the reburial (Naledzani Masala, 27; Mavis Naledzani, 30; Govan Mabirimisa, 26). The reburial underlined the importance of history to Venda culture (Ramudzuli Ludwig Muhadi). Although this was a welcome development, with local communities participating (Gladys Malindi Atshilovha, 35), some respondents were annoyed by the tussles between archaeologists, SANParks and government (Lucy Marubini, Godfrey Nephawe, 58; Mufungwa Mulaudzi, 28). Communication between the different stakeholders was characterised by poor dialogue (Mavhunga Pelwebe, 19).

Very strong opinions pointed out that no one could stop communities from searching their ancestors (Naledzani Alidzuli, 70). This is a very significant statement on communities engaging with and locating their pasts. Some indicated that the reburial exercise was long overdue (Munzhedzi Vele, Ludhere Fulufhelo, 19) and that it should have been conducted in 1994. One informant could not understand why 'white people' exhumed those human remains (Mothudi Shumani, 22). This reburial was a welcome event since it is a taboo to live with one's ancestral human remains unburied. It is also believed that one cannot succeed in life if their ancestral remains are publicly exposed. From a community point of view, this was a commemoration of the ancestors which never happened in the past (Ravele Pfuluwani, 30; Ramavhule Mukhode, 27). Whoever wants to excavate Mapungubwe in future must consult local, descendant communities directly connected with its past (Dephney Muselankoe, 25). Govan Mabirimisa (26) found it worrying when he heard that archaeologists during the 1930s excavated his ancestors without consulting anyone about it. One informant claimed he had not heard about the re-burial ceremony (Thabelo Muofhe, 19). Another pointed out that it was reasonable for archaeologists to exhume the human remains for research purposes (George Mudau, 36). Another indicated that the ceremonies were not in tandem with Venda traditions (Naledzani Thompho, 22).

4.5.8 *Traditions of Building in Stone*

An additional question was added to the questionnaire to ascertain whether some Venda communities still constructed their houses and cattle pens using stone. The responses were mixed. In some areas, this tradition seems to have been discontinued, e.g. in Thohoyandou, Mabirimisa and Mavbuka (Rendani Muletshothe, 23; Govan Mabirimisa, 26; Ludhere Fulufhelo, 19). The tradition may have been abandoned a decade or so ago, according to the estimates of one informant, although there are still such houses and cattle pens, which are no longer in use. In some areas you still have pole and daub houses, e.g. in Nzhelele, Dzimauli, Niani, Ha-Khakhu (Ravele Pfuluwani 30). In Mavhunga, only old stone houses are maintained (Fanie Marunzhe, 27). In areas regarded as very traditional such as Mutshekwa, they still build these structures (Thiathu Nicholus Madzhie, 30), as well as in Tshikwani tsha ha Mugobu, Tshipange, Mugobi) (Ramavhule Mukhode, 27), Ha-Miriri, (Mavhunga Pelwebe, 19), Kolawane village (Shumani Manenzhe, 21), Khunda, Niani, Phafuri and Tshandama villages (Radzilani Mulatedzi, 23). In other areas, stone is used in the design of modern buildings, e.g. at Ma-Tshavhawe (Fulufhelo Madumela, 30, Rendani Vhuhwavho, 24).

4.6 Conclusion

The various data presented in this chapter set a complex scenario, where archaeological heritage is presented outside the framework of descendant or claimant communities and the associated conservation challenges on the one hand, and the sites as claimed, 'owned' and 'accessed' by these communities on the other. The latter scenario points to a completely different perception in terms of approach towards cultural heritage management and conservation. The interpretation and analysis as presented in subsequent chapters stress that it is not the continuous unattended deterioration of archaeological sites that matters in heritage protection and conservation, but the presence of the spiritual values that these sites safeguard or represent, regardless of their appearance.

The reburial of Mapungubwe human remains is a significant exercise in a number of respects; it is a reminder to archaeologists and cultural heritage managers of the need by descendant communities to connect with the past in a spiritual sense; it may also be a case of communities inventing their own pasts or traditions (see Borofsky 1987; Evans 1985; Friedman 1992; Hughes and Trautmann 1995; Hobsbawm 1983; Peel 1984). Although traditional ceremonies were conducted to signify the events, there may have been nothing 'traditional' about the process, as the reburial exercise was a compromise. According to Hobsbawm and Ranger (1983), there are traditions which appear ancient, but instead are of recent origin, sometimes invented over a short period of time. Hobsbawm (1983) defines 'invented traditions' thus:

> 'Invented tradition' ... mean[s] a set of practices, normally governed by overtly or tacitly accepted rules and of a ritual or symbolic nature, which seek to inculcate certain values and norms of behaviour by repetition, which automatically implies continuity with the past. ...[W]here possible, they normally attempt to establish continuity with a suitable...past.... However, insofar as there is such reference to a ... past, the peculiarity of 'invented' traditions is that the continuity with it is largely fictitious. ... [T]hey are responses to novel situations which take the form of reference to old situations, or which establish their own past by quasi-obligatory repetition.

According to Hobsbawm (1983), 'invention' of tradition happens all the time and everywhere and more frequently during times of rapid social transformation when 'old' traditions are diminishing. What is regarded as 'new' traditions may have been invented over the past two centuries, in both 'traditional' and 'modern' societies, he argues. This also includes the re-invention, through revival, of extinct traditions. In the case of reburial of Mapungubwe remains, invented traditions would be those symbolizing specific group identities as well as social cohesion, as argued for by some Venda clans. This would serve as the basis for legitimizing the claim of Mapungubwe human remains and cementing the connection between the past and the present. Of interest in this study is how communities and the public at large find meaning and use the past in the present day. This is missing in contemporary cultural heritage studies, but crucial in understanding the relevance of the past to modern day societies. This is addressed in subsequent chapters.

CHAPTER FIVE
Data Analysis

5.1 Introduction

This chapter attempts to make sense of the data sets arising from this study— from oral interviews with communities, archaeological field surveys and the community engagement exercise involving negotiations and the process for the reburial of human remains excavated by archaeologists in the Mapungubwe Cultural Landscape. The data is qualitatively analysed in order to address the research questions raised in Chapter 2. The key issues are descendant communities' access to cultural heritage, understanding the meaning of cultural heritage, traditional or community perception of cultural heritage conservation, and sharing of cultural heritage information, in this context, archaeology, with non-archaeologists. Archaeologists have always worked with communities and the public, but of importance is the need to redefine and reconceptualise the relationship. Given a turbulent past characterised by racial discrimination and disrespect of the past of others, archaeologists in South Africa, the majority of whom are of European descent, are viewed with considerable mistrust, primarily for the work they have done on some archaeological sites that occupy a central place in community histories and memories of the past. The objective of this chapter is to underline the statement that cultural heritage protection should not be dictated from above as this will not provide adequate protection of archaeological sites. Instead, engagement of local and descendant communities is essential in achieving cultural heritage protection and ensuring a holistic understanding of heritage conservation.

5.2 Community Voices

The purpose of oral interviews was to assess the level of conservation awareness among communities in the Limpopo Province, specifically in Venda. Essentially, the purpose of conservation is to care for places of cultural heritage value, their structures, materials and meaning. In general, such places have lasting values and can be appreciated in their own right. They teach us about the past and the culture of our predecessors. They provide the context for community identity whereby people relate to the land and their ancestors. They provide variety and contrast in the modern world and a measure against which we can compare the achievements of today, as well as visible evidence of the continuity between past, present and future. Conservation thus helps us to understand the past and to protect cultural heritage. In view of the fact that archaeological cultural heritage conservation in South Africa has been carried out without involving mainly descendant communities, this project was designed to assess the level of non-involvement by communities. The questionnaire requested participants and the community they represented to give some indications on what researchers refer to as conservation of cultural resources. Of particular importance to this research was to determine how they, as individuals or community representatives, would like to see done in conserving archaeological sites as well as other sites of cultural/historical importance in the Limpopo Province. This would enable researchers to draft a programme of cultural (archaeological) heritage programme that will prioritise community participation or involvement in the management of cultural heritage. This was the basis for defining public or community archaeology— archaeologies practised in the public domain, with the consent and cooperation of communities and the public (Marshall 2009).

In this section, I make some qualitative assessments, based on the data presented in Chapter 4, on community awareness of conservation programmes in the Limpopo Province; what communities think about these programmes in general, and the levels of individual or community involvement in heritage conservation. Communities and individuals do want to be involved in heritage conservation in one way or the other, the compelling factor being employment and entrepreneurship, local development, and a sense of attachment with the past.

A majority of the informants indicated awareness of the conservation around a number of archaeological sites and landscapes in the Limpopo Province, and were quite positive that they enhance the protection of the sites/landscapes. However, the emphasis is that communities should be involved in nothing new in local South African (see Meskell 2007), African and global cultural heritage (see, Ndoro 2001). The most important commentary in my view is the critique that some of these conservation programmes tended to "freeze" cultural heritage, instead of creating a living past. The informant who raised this point was not even referring to the Mapungubwe Cultural Landscape, but the conservation programmes in Venda. His point may be connected to comments from a member of the Ga-Machete Royal family, who, during the reburial exercise, and in an informal discussion, indicated to me that conservation programmes in the area covered by the Mapungubwe Cultural Landscape were not people-centred, but instead focused on wild animals and vegetation. This is a significant critique on current conservation efforts, which are rooted in developments of the 1920s and the 1930s. The proposed Limpopo/Shashe Transfrontier Conservation Area (TFCA) straddling the international borders of Botswana, South Africa and Zimbabwe is an outcome of this development (see Map 3). I discuss this in detail in thwe following paragraphs to indicate how current conservation efforts are essentially preclusive rather than inclusive of descendant communities, and hence, an impediment of access to cultural heritage, mainly archaeological, in the area.

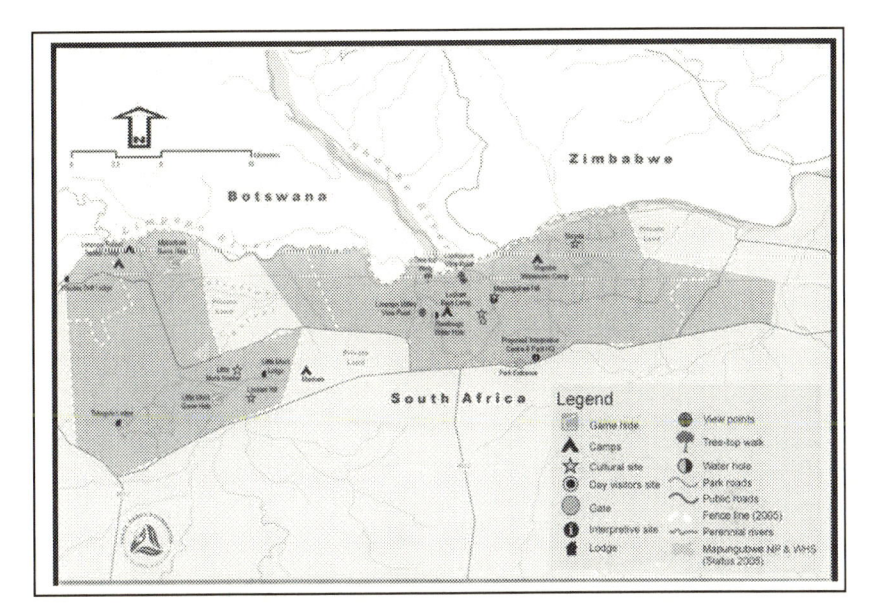

Map 3: The Mapungubwe National Park and World Heritage Landscape (Courtesy of Peace Parks Foundation)

The proposed TFCA subsumes land that belongs to different stakeholders in an effort to create a conservation initiative that involves partnerships between the three governments, landowners in the area and local communities, the latter of whom live in areas peripheral to the park. The area teems with substantial amounts of wildlife (Alcock 1988; Selier 2007), has a unique geology and physiography (Mason 1973), and very well known and important archaeological sites (Calabrese 2005; Fouche 1937; Gardner 1963; Huffman 2002, 2005 and 2007; Schoeman 2006; Smith 2005). As such, the TFCA includes both nature and culture.

Environmentalists, mainly through the World Conservation Union (IUCN), have since the 1980s identified more than 100 protected areas that swath across common international boundaries. Since these share so many things in common, the advantages of bringing them together in terms of inter-governmental objectives, common conservation approaches and local community engagement are abundant. Interestingly, the idea behind the establishment of a conservation area straddling the extensive Shashe-Limpopo confluence is not new. It dates from the early 1920s when General Jan Smuts ordered a number of farms along the Limpopo River to be set aside for the Dongola Botanical Reserve, adjacent to the frontiers of the then Bechuanaland Protectorate and Southern Rhodesia. The objective behind such a reserve was to study the vegetation and assess the agricultural and pastoral potential of the area. This led to the creation of the Dongola National Park in the 1940s when feasibility studies suggested that the area was not suitable for human habitation and that it could best be used as a "wildlife sanctuary for the recreation of the nation" (Carruthers 1992 and 2006).

The size of the proposed TFCA is nearly 140,000 hectares, and comprises the northern Tuli Game Reserve in Botswana; private farms, state land, land owned by mining giants (De Beers Consolidated Mines Ltd), national parks (SANParks), and non-governmental organisations (Peace Parks Foundation) in South Africa, and the Tuli Circle in Zimbabwe. This area teems with wildlife. It is predominantly elephant country, with numbers exceeding 1400 (Selier 2007). Their management involves periodic culling and hunting. Other wild animals include the leopard, lion, hyena, giraffe, antelope, cheetah and wildebeest, some of which are hunted for their meat and skins. The Limpopo and its tributaries are also home to several species of bird and crocodile.

Current efforts towards the realisation of the TFCA include the integration in 2002 of 40,000 hectares owned by De Beers by establishing the Venetia Limpopo Nature Reserve; since 2004, land purchases from private landowners and consolidation into what is now the Mapungubwe National Park, and the possibility of incorporating portions of the Maramani Communal Lands into the conservation area. This development is done in phases, as it is impossible to acquire the necessary properties at once, with the objective of eventually linking all the three countries.

Although efforts to include communities in the conservation area are being explored, the most compelling factor is the potential for a "big five" — lion, leopard, elephant, rhinoceros, and the buffalo. The De Beers Venetia Wildlife Conservation Project seeks to conserve bio-diversity, restore natural ecological processes and develop ecologically and economically sound landuse practices. The aim is to provide benefits and opportunities, primarily through tourism, for the region and its resident communities. These objectives are in congruence with the management objectives of the Mapungubwe National Park, and in partial fulfilment of the proposed trans-frontier conservation area.

The archaeological richness of the area that will fall under the proposed TFCA is immense, with a very long history of research (Gardner 1955, 1958, 1963; Hall and Smith 2000; Huffman 2000 and 2007; Manyanga 2007; Mason 1962; Mothulatshipi 2009; van Riet Lowe 1936; Voigt 1983), and recent ethno-history (Bonner and Curruthers 2003; Hofmeyer 1989; van Warmelo 1942). It is this cultural significance that is connected with community claims on Mapungubwe as well as recent successful land claims by some Venda clans. The claims should be viewed as attempts by communities to negotiate access to cultural heritage resources. Such attempts are made difficult by current conservation efforts, which, although situated in the broader global context of developments around trans-frontier conservation and cultural landscapes (see Fowler 2003 and 2004), have serious historical antecedents. I also realised, when I posed questions about traditional methods and ceremonies necessary in cultural heritage conservation that communities saw conservation as only happening or occurring within a specific cultural setting, involving local beliefs and practices. Thus Western approaches to conservation of archaeological sites in the research area can only succeed in consultation with local elders, spiritual and traditional leaders connected with those sites. Non-involvement of descendant communities is futile and alienates the sites or landscapes in question.

5.3 Condition Assessments and Cultural Heritage Conservation

Condition assessments were only conducted at the stone walled site in Ratho Farm and the midden of Bambandyanalo (K2) to determine the primary threats to site preservation. Prior documentation of condition surveys in the Limpopo Province was only accessed for the stonewalled site of Dzata in Venda. This is the only site where attempts to integrate conservation with local, descendant community knowledge were done in the past, though this seems not the objective of the documentation exercise.

5.3.1 *Dzata*

The stonewalled site of Dzata (see Map 2 and Figure 25) is the 18th century capital of the legendary Venda leader Thohoyandou, who according to Stayt (1931) and van Warmelo (1932), was related to the Rozvi of Zimbabwe. It has been studied by archaeologists (Huffman 1996; Hanisch 2008) and historians (Ralushai and Gray 1977). Huffman (1996, 40) gives a full plan of the palace (after Loubser 1992) and a plan of what he refers to as the audience chamber.

Fig. 25. The Site of Dzata (Photo by the Author)

My assessment of conservation of the site is solely based on the July 2004 2nd *Technical Course on Inventory and Documentation of Immovable Cultural Heritage* course sponsored by AFRICA 2009 in partnership with UNESCO World Heritage Centre, ICCROM, and CRATerre-EAG. Programme participants did a basic manual documentation and mapping of the site. They also identified threats to the site on the maps they produced and those in existing documentation. These threats as well as features missing on existing maps were recorded and mapped on new site plans. In this way, course participants were able to amend missing architectural and other features.

Intangible heritage was also documented and attempts were made to map it. Intangible heritage is critical in understanding immovable heritage. Locations associated with various aspects of intangible heritage were identified with the assistance of local communities from the nearby village (see p.22 of the report). Interesting results emerging from the documentation exercise were clearly identifiable differences between archaeologists' and local communities' interpretation of the site.

What is surprising is that the mapping of intangible heritage was not regarded as part of condition assessment, which was carried out separately from the overall site conservation exercise. Using photographs, text descriptions, mapping and graphic representations, the condition survey exercise was able to identify and report on signs of wall decay, erosion, destroyed or deformed walls, areas of recent damage. A detailed site inventory as well as a condition survey report for the site was produced as part of the documentation exercise. It emerged from the documentation that one needed to understand the type of heritage before any condition survey is undertaken. Little to poor knowledge of a specific heritage may result in incorrect diagnosis and wrong intervention solutions. For condition surveys for a site such as Dzata, an understanding of the character of dry stone walls found in southern Africa is important (see Ndoro 2001). It was on the basis of this recommendation that condition surveys or assessments were conducted at the stone walled structure at Ratho Farm.

5.3.2 *The Stonewalled Site on Ratho Farm*

The stonewalled site on Ratho Farm is one of several sites of this type in the middle Limpopo Valley and areas extending south towards the Soutpansberg Mountains. These sites are associated with post-Mapungubwe developments, the spread of the Zimbabwe Culture in this region, specifically during the last three centuries, and Venda origin histories (Huffman and Hanisch 1987). Situated on a domed sandstone hill overlooking the Limpopo-Motloutse confluence area, the site in question is interpreted as a regional capital. It is composed of neatly coursed free-standing curvilinear stone walls to the south and south-east (though wall extensions extending to the west are comparatively poor in terms of coursing) and a small enclosure with rubble wall incorporating a neatly coursed stonewalled platform (Figure 26; see also Chapter 4 for detailed wall sections). Settlement activity in terms of houses is not very visible within the enclosed area. Huffman and Hanisch (1987, 102) interpret the site as specifically used for initiation ceremonies, but the basis for such an interpretation rests on thin evidence.

The condition assessment carried on the site was designed to identify the core threats to sites which do not receive any monitoring at all, other than the overarching protection based on the site being located within a private farm. On the basis of the observations recorded, these sites do confront accelerated deterioration regardless of their location. The main threats to Ratho were structural weaknesses, leading to bulges, displacement of rocks and toppling, instability of core material resulting in some walls sinking, deterioration of individual blocks; splitting, causing walls to become loose and crumble. Wild animals, specifically baboons, are responsible for some of these structural problems.

Fig. 26. The Fairly Neatly Coursed Free Standing Stonewalls at Ratho (Photo by the Author).

While it is recommended that this site is attended to in order to reverse the deterioration of stone and other visible archaeological structures, more detailed documentation of the site is preferred to assess the conditions of the wall over time. The map provided by Huffman and Hanisch (1987, 93 and 103) and the photographs taken during field surveys in 2006, 2007, and 2008 are useful in this regard as a basis for an intensive documentation study. Of concern to archaeologists and cultural heritage managers is the deterioration of the site towards 'rubble', while for descendant communities, it is this state of presentation that actually defines the presence of ancestors (Dr Munyaradzi Manyanga, pers comm. 2008). This indicates that heritage professionals view conservation of cultural heritage places very differently from communities closely associated with those places.

Are condition surveys an integral part of traditional conservation practices? The site of Thimlich Ohinga in the Nyanza Province of Kenya seems to have been periodically maintained through such surveys. Onjala and Kamaru (2005) mention that apart from the prohibitive taboos that formed some of the laws protecting the stonewalled site, the chief and elders of the communities took the responsibility of ensuring and protecting the stonewalls. Site residents had to respect the walls as these structures were linked to the ancestral world and were therefore spiritual. Interactions with the structure were regulated and guided in such a way that will not offend the spirit world. Thimlich Ohinga was maintained and repaired, and this involved regular inspection and monitoring, assessment of the structural problems, the mobilization of labour and the necessary resources to do the repair work. It was the responsibility of each resident including the chief and elders to routinely inspect the site and report the problem, if any, e.g. potential wall collapses, fallen walls, etc. If necessary, experts would be called to make proper diagnosis of the problem and assist with repairs or maintenance work. Normally, this was a community-driven exercise (Onjala and Kamaru 2005).

5.3.3 *Bambandyanalo* (K2)

Bambandyanalo site is being monitored as part of the SANParks stabilization programme (Nienaber and Hutten 2006). This programme has been designed to reduce threats caused by erosion, soil creep and wild animals compacting archaeological deposits by creating an environment conducive towards the growth of grass. It is expected that this would keep the very fragile archaeological deposits intact.

Archival photos of this site as well as Mapungubwe Hill show considerable scarring on the surface due to the open stripping, extensive excavations by previous investigators (See Chapter 4 for details on site plans). This is slowly being eclipsed by the nature of refilling from the stabilisation programme.

The rehabilitation exercise on such an extensive midden presents such a considerable challenge, given the increased number of wild animals in the park. The quantity of grass growing on the ashy deposits is unsubstantial to lessen the rate of soil erosion currently taking place. It is the frailty of the archaeological deposits that compels heritage managers to close the site from the public. This renders an interpretive centre built there as a past of a site presentation derelict (see Figure 27). This is compounded by poor access roads, which easily convert into gullies with every flooding/hill wash.

Fig. 27. The Fragility of the Archaeological Deposits of the Type Found at K2 Is Demonstrated by Efforts to Stabilize Them as Shown in This Picture (Photo courtesy of Johan Nel).

Some of the human remains were re-buried on this site. Of concern to cultural heritage managers is the aesthetic presentation of the site.

5.4 Reburial in the Context of Archaeological Knowledge Production

In 2006 and 2007, the University of Pretoria and the South African Department of Environmental Affairs and Tourism were engaged by communities from the Limpopo Province and other stakeholders, specifically Venda clans and representatives of San communities to repatriate the human remains excavated from Mapungubwe, Bambandyanalo and other sites. While the sticking points in the negotiations were getting the various clans to agree on the process of return and eventual reburial of these remains, and while the university was eager to correct the wrongs committed by its researchers in the past in the quest for best cultural heritage practice in the post-apartheid context, I listened to some of the points raised during the consultative meetings, which encapsulate community expectations on how archaeological knowledge should be shared. These expectations, if adopted in future research, could serve to define the role post-colonial and post-apartheid archaeology should play in the knowledge society. Some of the points include:

i. *How the teaching of the past could be made more inclusive and reflect the histories of local communities.* Current archaeological reports, though presenting some informative regional coverage, have engaged with issues of group identity which do not relate to local clan histories (Huffman 2007).

ii. *The role of the media in engaging the public in matters relating to the past.* Both radio and television seem to go for 'expert' opinion on issues pertaining to interpretation and presentation of the past, and as a result, local community voices are ignored or silenced.

iii. *The role of memory, archaeology and tradition.* Although memory has become a prolific area of enquiry in history and archaeology, this is largely absent in the study and interpretation of Mapungubwe and other sites in the Limpopo Province of South Africa. Although social memory is disparate, located and fragmented, it serves to challenge authoritative, dominant, but at the same time highly contested narratives about the past of these communities. The rich Venda oral traditions, origin myths and folktales remain poorly exploited for purposes of archaeological research, but there is considerable potential. The stonewalled archaeological heritage in the Limpopo Province has played a considerable role in the production of Venda oral histories and social memory (see Hanisch 2008). What communities expect from this is a platform to challenge competing post-apartheid and postcolonial narratives about their pasts.

iv. *The need to develop a research agenda that takes into account community and academic interests*— this involves working together to define research projects and approaches to address certain issues of the past, such as histories of origins and development of some clans. This request comes after realising that researchers and heritage managers have the final say in the interpretation and presentation of the past.

v. *The 'silencing' and 'closure' of Mapungubwe and the need for communities to be granted increased access to the newly proclaimed World Heritage site and associated cultural landscape.* This is comparable to current concerns by Karanga clans living around Great Zimbabwe (Fontein 2006).

Some of these expectations are a challenge to the dominance and overarching nature of colonial and apartheid archaeology, which tend to treat local and regional histories in terms of material culture patterning and sequencing, largely devoid of known historical entities. This 'silent' approach towards the presentation of the past is an anathema to sharing knowledge between professionals and non-professionals, and not useful in protecting those sites we seek to study.

5.5 Reburial and Tradition

As detailed in Chapter 4, the reburial exercise involved a cleansing ceremony at Mapungubwe Hill, a public ceremony to celebrate the reburial at the confluence of the Shashe and Limpopo rivers, and the reburial of the human remains.

The human remains were packed in high density polyurethane boxes to ensure that the remains would stay well-preserved for as long as possible. According to Nienaber *et al.* (2008), this polyurethane can last up to 400 years if not exposed to any form of thermal or chemical influences. During the reburial ceremony, communities accompanied the 'miniature coffins' from a temporary storage facility to the place of burial. This was marked by ritual and ceremony, involving singing and oration.

The reburial took place at the summit of Mapungubwe Hill, at Bambandyanalo (K2), Schroda, and near the new interpretation centre, all sites within the Mapungubwe Cultural Landscape. The grave shafts were initially excavated, and constructed of brick walls and cement. The manhole was then covered with a concrete slab, with a manhole in the middle for future access, if required. The reburial places or structures coincided as much as possible with the archaeological contexts from which some of these remains were originally excavated. For Bambandyanalo, the reburial was done in Gardner 1936–39 Test Trench (Meyer 1988; Gardner 1963), while at Mapungubwe, the reburial took place in the trench excavated by Neville Jones and Schofield in 1934 Trench 5 (JS 5) (Fouche 1937).

The question is whether the reburial conducted was in accordance with the traditions of the various communities participating in the process. Judging from the sentiments of some communities, e.g. the Machete, were of the view that proper rituals and ceremonies had not been followed. Various individuals were of the view that the reburial ceremony has succeeded in bringing the ancestors of the communities back home. Others felt that the process was a compromise and that archaeologists still held sway over the remains. They accurately pointed out to the creation of the roof concrete slab as primarily designed for anyone who would want to study the remains in the future, and not just as an exercise in conserving the human remains.

5.6 Conclusion

This research shows that in applying modern conservation approaches to cultural heritage places, we often ignore community knowledge about how these places were 'abandoned' and the cultural meaning of such leaving processes in terms of site conservation. Archaeologists obliterate a range of human behaviours, often reducing complex processes to simple or non-events. While communities did abandon such places in the past, oral information tells us that human-land relationships implied that they did not give up claims to places they had settled originally. This is demonstrated by continued use of some of these sites in the present.

Non-Western views on cultural heritage conservation must be given serious attention. To the heritage professional, they may appear, at face value, 'non-rational' but the objective behind these is to preserve the social value of heritage, including protecting intangible values. We might ask at this juncture the role of ritual, ceremony and tradition in the conservation of cultural heritage. The only literature that addressed this question is Cisse (2005), whose research on the Dogon people of Mali demonstrated an intricate relationship between mythology, cosmology and their physical manifestation through ceremonial centres. The annual Bulo ceremony of Arou in north-eastern Mali endow Dogon heritage with a conservation dynamic that is well defined in the peoples' worldview— preserving a category of immovable heritage, including temples, sanctuaries and grain storehouses. This important anthropological research topic is worth pursuing (see Fontein 2006, in the case of Great Zimbabwe).

Fig. 28. The Biological Diversity within the Mapungubwe Cultural Landscape (Photo by the Author).

The issue of access to heritage resources, as demanded by some descendants communities lies in the perceived conflict between culture and biodiversity (Figure 28), often pitting environmentalists against the new thinking in cultural heritage management that advocates for increased community and public participation. Mapungubwe National Park and World Heritage Landscape is rich in biological diversity and SANParks are making a concerted effort to preserve it. Being located on the periphery of South Africa, and also being part of the borderlands of Botswana and Zimbabwe, no one would imagine this pristine land would come under threats or experience potential biodiversity loss. The causes of biodiversity loss are habitat loss and fragmentation, often through clearance of native vegetation for agriculture, human settlement and industrial development; invasive alien species, which may be introduced on purpose or by accident; pollution which poisons all forms of terrestrial and marine life, and climate change. The effects of the last are now beginning to be appreciated, though discussions remain controversial, cyclical and inconclusive. Over exploitation of some areas also contributes to biodiversity loss as humans end up destroying natural ecosystems. The rapid growth of human population as well as poorly monitored illegal border crossing and wildlife hunting are therefore a major point of concern to SANParks and conservationists. In the Mapungubwe National Park and the adjacent buffer zone, a major point of worry is the rapid growth of elephant populations on the one hand and the exploitation of the area by mining companies for diamonds and coal, on the other. Environmentalists think such developments will compromise the environmental integrity of the area in and around a world heritage setting, and thus threaten generations to come. Recently, non-governmental organisations, groups and associations such as the Endangered Wildlife Trust (EWT), the Peace Parks Foundation (PPF), the Association of Southern African Professional Archaeologists (ASAPA), the Mapungubwe Action Group (MAG), the Wilderness Foundation South Africa (the WFSA), the World Wide Fund for Nature South Africa (the WWF) and BirdLife South Africa (BLSA), have lodged an appeal against a new, opencast coal mine, which was granted licence to mine near Mapungubwe. By siding with the environmentalists, archaeologists have in the process perpetuated the mistrust communities continue to have over them, as the latter perceive development not as a threat to cultural heritage or biodiversity, but to their very own existence, in a world confronted by serious poverty.

CHAPTER SIX

Data Interpretation: Archaeology and Communities in the Present

6.1 Introduction

This chapter subsumes the data presented and analyzed in the previous chapters to provide wide ranging interpretations. The research questions raised in Chapter 2 are also addressed here in the broader context of the heritage discourse. To minimize conflict between professionals, in this case, heritage managers and local communities, I also discuss how the past may be shared between them. The discussion also realizes that although the term cultural heritage is used substantially in archaeological circles, its meaning is parochial primarily for management of sites and landscapes. I would like to use this term to address what I refer to in this study as 'tradition'. Traditions are distinct group or culture-specific beliefs, customs, ritualistic and ceremonial practices transmitted over generations, in most cases through word of mouth. Their preservation and retention is conditioned by and through social interaction. Anyone— individual, family, society— can be a guardian of tradition, either consciously or unconsciously, and in the process, contribute towards their preservation or demise. Continued preservation and practice of certain tradition, through ritual and ceremony, creates an accepted corpus of knowledge, thus it is knowledge production, and is important in providing an understanding of a group or culture. It is the forced disjuncture between the past and present— the severance of tradition— that has resulted in the conflict between heritage managers, archaeologists and descendant communities. These conflicting positions may be resolved through sharing of 'tradition' with the 'present'.

6.2 Understanding Cultural Heritage

A major question arising from this research is how communities understand cultural heritage. The notion of heritage offers a language through which to discuss contested issues of culture and identity, among others, in a post-colonial context, and hovers between individual and collective conceptions of history and sits uneasily between past and present (Shephered 2008). Discussion of the term 'heritage' among a range of disciplines including history, anthropology, archaeology, and other social sciences, reveals a complex set of issues arising from attempts to understand its meaning or meanings. According to Watkins and Beaver (2008), the term draws on an idea of an inherited legacy, has its roots in the past and continues to be meaningful in the present.

When discussing cultural heritage, we often resort to the definition used by UNESCO, which perceives it as "...our legacy from the past, what we live with today, and what we pass on to future generations" (King 2008a; Ndoro 2008) or simply "cultural resources", a term mainly used in the USA. The Western perception of heritage dichotomised it into the domains of culture and nature (see Lowenthal 2005), heritage as archive, heritage as museum, heritage as tourism, as an economic resource, etc. This 'fragmentation' of the term is also problematic (Guillaume 1980). A recent discussion among the members of the World Archaeological Congress (WAC) questioned the term cultural heritage as used in archaeology and related disciplines. It emerged from the discussions how fluid the term was in ascribing it identity and ownership. Indigenous peoples aside, questions were raised why some currently existing groups of people have to call the remains of past people part of their heritage. The discussion explored the possibilities of using appropriate theoretical and methodological approaches for understanding cultural heritage and for a comprehensive definition of the term.

The term "cultural resources" as used in North America implies things that can be used, and that are somehow related to "culture", those aspects of the environment—both physical and intangible, both natural and built—that have cultural value to specific groups of people and communities. According to King (2003), the term should include those non-material human social institutions that help make up our social institutions, our beliefs, our accustomed practices, and our perceptions of what makes the environment culturally comfortable. When we use the term "resource", we are also implying some broader 'usefulness' beyond the general cultural good of such evidence of past and current value. However, archaeologists use the term in a narrow sense to mean "archaeological sites" or "historic monuments". Therefore archaeologists are always dealing with a very narrow concept of heritage, which is reduced further to 'dots on the map', rather than a landscape with overlapping layers of cultural meaning. There is need to take into consideration the significance of landscapes as cultural heritage/systems and the way in which sites interconnect and reveal the former use of the environment. Untold systems of knowledge have disappeared from view in this manner and have led to the credulous objectification of cultural heritage as a series of 'sites' or objects or myth fragments (see, McDonald, Coldrick and Villiers 2005). King (2002) suggests that we should look beyond archaeological sites to include other types of properties such as cultural landscapes, historical records, social institutions, expressive cultures, old buildings, religious beliefs and practices, rituals and ceremonies, and folk life. What we then refer to as cultural resources management (CRM) is, or implies, managing the impacts of the modern world on these resources (King 2003). In archaeology, we are also implying the impact of archaeological excavations on some of these places.

There are suggestions that cultural heritage should comprise all places and occasions at/on which the past of a given culture is collectively remembered (Holtorf 2005 and 2007) but others consider this too ethereal. Heritage should not be restricted to cultural memory as there are previously unknown sites and material remains found as a result of archaeological research which have become heritage. Archaeology has not been very visible in the broader field of heritage studies, when compared to history, anthropology, and related disciplines.

Attempting to define what cultural heritage "is" is perhaps a self-defeating exercise, and instead a better perception should focus on understanding how heritage works in any given cultural and historical context. A broader definition, in my view, would be preferable where heritage is always viewed in plural terms due to its diversity contingency, context-sensitivity and fluidity. Heritage is not only about objects, sites or other things (see King 2002)— it is also about the cultural processes and performances of management, conservation/preservation and commemoration. We need to move away from a purely object-centred concern for heritage as evidenced by the 2003 Intangible Cultural Heritage Convention, a development heavily influenced by archaeologists, historians and cultural heritage managers from Africa and other non-Western cultures. In this study, heritage is considered central to the very definition of what it means to be part of a culture and way of life. It has a perplexing scope in meanings and uses because it can be applied to just about anything that has value for a community or group as part of its identity, sense of belonging, and things that properly belong to the group. Heritage is not just "the past" but is a "lived present", which is used and celebrated (Pikirayi 2006 and 2011). The reburial exercise at Mapungubwe has also shown that heritage is tradition and that it is through tradition that the past is conserved and protected. In this way, heritage is also a way of interacting with others in the same environment and beyond (see the OSEA, The Open School of Ethnography and Anthropology perception of heritage as presented in www.osea-cite.org/what_is_heritage.php). According to King (2008b), "...cultural heritage is a group of resources inherited from the past which people identify, independently of ownership, as a reflection and expression of their constantly evolving values, beliefs, knowledge and traditions. It includes all aspects of the environment resulting from the interaction between people and places through time". This may play into ethnic or nationalist agendas at various levels of community or society, and therefore heritage is not apolitical (Aplin 2002).

Many scholars are of the opinion that tradition is something that asserts that if people are to maintain their socio-cultural identities, they must accept certain behaviour patterns that are required of them (Boonzaier and Spiegel 2008). In my view the term does not imply a 'return' to the past. Rather, from the data presented in the previous chapter, it seems that appeals to tradition are in effect people's efforts to adapt to the contestations and competitive demands of the modern world. This is tandem with King's (2002 and 2003) understanding of cultural resources and their management.

6.3 Contemporary Use of Sites and Cultural Landscapes

The data presented in Chapter 4 also demonstrated that communities claim use and access to certain heritage places and landscapes, and these claims are not governed by who the 'rightful owner' of those cultural resources are, but instead by accepted forms of knowledge and traditions.

The date of the abandonment of Mapungubwe, according to the archaeological evidence, is 1290 AD (Huffman 2007). This creates a disjunction between the past and present to the extent that it has been argued that Venda speakers are not direct descendants of the people who once lived at Mapungubwe. This placed major legal obstacles on Venda communities who were making a claim of the human remains excavated from Mapungubwe, Bambandyanalo and other sites nearby. Such legal arguments do not consider the validity of cultural memory and tradition in contemporary use and ownership of cultural heritage sites and landscapes. The stories connected with the 're-discovery' of Mapungubwe in the late 19th and early 20th centuries contradict this perception:

The story of a certain Mowena— leading to the 'discovery' of the treasures on Mapungubwe Hill by Jerry van Graan in 1932 and the subsequent systematic research by the University of Pretoria (Fouche 1937; Gardner 1955 and 1963)— is both an adventure of European dealings (Curruthers 2006) with the remote 'frontier' and an encounter between 'modernity' and 'tradition'. Firstly Mowena refused to part with an unusual ceramic container, which Jerry had offered to buy because the pot came from a 'sacred hill' near the Limpopo River. During that time, the site was regarded as 'the burial place of the natives' including 'the chief's grave'. This ceramic container then became a mnemonic device for Jerry, since he remembered the story of the hermit Francois Bernard Lotrie, who around 1890, lived around that hill, from where he found and plundered a treasure comprising gold and other precious artefacts. Mowena was eventually forced to show Jerry the hill, on which summit he found large quantities of golden objects including bangles, beads, nails and a miniature buffalo (Fouche 1937). They also found a rhino, human skeletal remains and gold anklets.

What is evident from this story is that there has been 'tradition' about the sacred nature of Mapungubwe which was not supposed to be shared to outsiders in order to safeguard the site from plunder. The moment sacredness was compromised, the site experienced untold pillage in the form gold objects being taken by the Van Graans family and their neighbours who had farms in the area. The making of the findings at Mapungubwe public in 1933 with the help of General Jan Smuts (a conservator) and the intervention by the University of Pretoria to 'save' the archaeological site was just another exercise in alienating the place, since the University was to commence a programme of systematic excavations—which entail destruction! Mapungubwe's links with its own past, and its conservation in traditional terms were effectively lost.

Mapungubwe has already acquired some kind of 'centrality' in South Africa, primarily because of its archaeology. Although Mapungubwe is located in the northern part of South Africa, on the Shashe and Limpopo confluence, it plays a central role in the country. The site is 'alive' today and features prominently in South Africa's annual national heritage celebrations. The main reasons for this are the values for which it has been recognized as a national monument as well as a world heritage cultural landscape. The Mapungubwe landscape contains evidence for an important interchange of human values that resulted in significant cultural and social changes in the southern African region between AD 900 and 1300. There is archaeological evidence of the existence of a society which, at the time, was the largest in the region. This society had trading connections with eastern Africa and Asia, confirming the evidence of an exchange of human values. Scientists have also documented climate change in the area, used by archaeologists to model the growth and demise of the kingdom that was based at Mapungubwe Hill. This centrality of Mapungubwe features in many usable ways in contemporary South Africa (Pikirayi 2009). While archaeology is important in its own way as subject that informs us about the past, it has been criticised in this instance for distancing descendant communities from cultural heritage which they regard as theirs.

The most important point to emerge from this study is that, firstly, descendant communities are connected to the archaeological sites in the research area, and, secondly, the past is usable. Such usable pasts are driven by historical and cultural experiences such as losses experienced by some nations and ethnic groups as a result of enslavement, colonisation, wars, racial segregation, massacres or genocides, much of which is fixed in people's memories (Roskies 1999). South Africa is no exception given its violent past.

6.4 Traditional Conservation of Archaeological Sites

Mapungubwe Hill, Bambandyanalo and Schroda have recently been conserved under the SANParks poverty alleviation programme (Nienaber and Hutten 2006). The conservation exercise or programme mainly involved stabilisation of exposed archaeological deposits so as to save the fragile deposits buried underneath. This has successfully been carried out, though regular monitoring and assessment is required to ensure that the sites in question are preserved for posterity.

Conservation of cultural landscapes is always tied up with the worldviews of the descendant communities linked with those cultural landscapes (see Kankpeyeng (2005) for the case of the Tongo Hills, home of the Talensi, in northern Ghana; and Githitho (2005) for the Mijikenda Kaya or fortified forests of coastal Kenya). Conservation of such places is normally governed by traditional rules and prohibitions passed down by descendant communities from generation to generation. In case where such landscapes may be abandoned for one reason or another, they assume ritual and ceremonial importance, with descendant communities viewing them as symbols of their cultural identity. This is because attachment to place is not lost due to abandonment. These landscapes, according to descendant communities' worldview, remain the dwelling places of their ancestors who were buried there. Destruction of such places is strictly prohibited as this implies desecration. There are rules relating to physical maintenance of a place as well as rules relating to behaviour and activities within particular places. The primary objective was to conserve the spiritual importance of the place or landscape.

In much of southern Africa, archaeological sites are not 'abandoned' places, but residential places of ancestors, precursors of the living. According to both Karanga[2] and Venda worldviews, these places are owned by ancestors, whose spirits reside there. While communities did literally leave sites or regions for other places during pre-colonial times, human-land relationships implied that they did not give up claims to places they had settled originally. If they did so, they would be abandoning the dead, specifically their ancestors. The major conflict in southern Africa between archaeology as a Western science and tradition is that archaeologists often perceive abandonment in terms of sites no longer used or occupied, while local or indigenous communities attach spiritual values around such places. These challenges have confronted heritage managers, particularly when communities ask for access to such places to honour their ancestors or conduct rituals and ceremonies that link them with their pasts. In this section, I discuss some Karanga worldviews to understand the local notion of archaeological site— *dongo* [singular, plural – *matongo*]— and the accretion of concepts of spirituality and intangibility around such places. The objective is to understand why local communities place value on such places, especially when their dead are buried in or around them.

6.4.1 Background

In 2006, my colleague and I presented a paper entitled "Archaeology and conflict of values— a postcolonial ethical perspective on the archaeology of 'death' in southern Africa" at the Association of Southern African Professional Archaeologists (ASAPA) biennial conference in Pretoria. Focusing on burial archaeology, our argument, in essence was that any discussion on ethics in southern African archaeology must necessarily consider the history of the discipline. Antiquarian plunder of

---

[2] Some traditions claim Venda origins from the southern Zimbabwe plateau, across the Limpopo River. Karanga is a southern dialect cluster of people referred to as Shona, and shares close linguistic affinities with Venda (Beach 1980).

archaeological sites had earlier on triggered conflicts between descendant communities and researchers, as the interests of the latter could not be reconciled with the interests of the former. Subsequent to this, professional archaeologists failed to incorporate indigenous African values into their code of practice. They took advantage of the colonial context to gather their data, which included human skeletal remains. We cited the prime examples of Ingombe Ilede (Fagan, Phillipson and Daniels 1969) and Sanga (de Maret 1982), a Mapungubwe (Meyer 1998), whose unearthing yielded rich burials and other artefacts, all for the benefit of research (see Steyn 1997 and 1998; Steyn and Henneberg 1995 and 1996). We pointed out that the archaeologists responsible did not take into account the cultural importance of traditional, non-European burials. We also pointed out that in contemporary archaeology in southern Africa, the so-called 'archaeology of death' (Chapman and Randsborg 1981; Hubert and Fjorde 2002; Fforde 2004; Pearson 2003; Humphreys and King 1981) only served a limited audience, and consequently alienated the discipline from the public. We proposed that archaeologists adopt approaches that were in tandem with indigenous values, lest their discipline loses academic and social relevance.

Judging from the responses of the audience, dominated by white South African archaeologists, our paper received a hostile reception. It was perceived as an attack on white archaeologists, among other allegations of trying to politicise a discipline that should simply be regarded as a science. Coming at a time when South African communities were increasingly calling for the return and reburial of human remains excavated by archaeologists from sites which they regard as ancestral (Nienaber 2007; Nienaber and Steyn 2002; Nienaber *et al.* 2008), we caused considerable disquiet amongst our ranks. Since then, considerable change of attitude has taken place in South African archaeology, not because of our paper, but because of persistent calls within the leadership of ASAPA to embrace a transformation agenda and plan of action in archaeology that would change not only the demographics, but also approaches to the study of the past. This would mean embracing archaeologies that are relevant to the public in general, and, especially, to descendant communities. The latter, in my opinion, are most negatively affected by what archaeologists do, particularly the excavation and exhumation of human remains, their use in academic research, and display in museums. In this section I emphasise two points. Archaeologists in southern Africa must broaden their perception of archaeological sites to embrace intangibility, especially aspects of spirituality so as to minimize potential conflict with the public and indigenous communities. Any attempts to conserve a site excavated of its human remains are invalid if such values are not acknowledged.

6.4.2 *Archaeology and Intangibility*

To understand the worldview of the living and their dead ancestors in Africa and much of the world, some of the issues raised by the International Council on Monuments and Sites (ICOMOS) General Assembly and Scientific Symposium held at Victoria Falls in October 2003 in connection with the intricate links between tangible and intangible heritage as subsequently adopted by UNESCO are relevant (Gonçalves *et al.* 2003). The discussions upheld the principle deeply ingrained in ideas of site significance in most parts of Africa, namely, that tangible and intangible heritage are inseparable aspects. The intangible heritage provides the spirit and confirmation of the values and significance of a place. It is this aspect of heritage that is missing on most sites archaeologists work on because of land alienation. Munjeri (2004) has pointed out that most instances of the destruction or loss of intangible heritage occurred out of total ignorance of the value of sites, objects and associated practices, and it is the long-term non-purposeful neglect that is the most serious.

Since intangibility is context specific, it is difficult to define (see Kirshenblatt-Gimblett 2004). The 2003 Victoria Falls meeting succeeded in drawing up theoretical definitions and concepts about the spirit of a place that evolved through work in many parts of the world. The various ideas on intangibility confronted Western approaches that perceive heritage through tangible values and yet conservation of historical sites is supported by many intangible aspects, such as conservation of the memory of events. Both tangible and intangible values must therefore be assessed in relation to the evolution and history of place (Gonçalves *et al.* 2003).

The sacred nature of sites is important in the context of intangibility. Continuity of ceremony and ritual in such spaces guarantees maintenance of intangible values. Change through time in such practices happens, conditioned by various circumstances some of which may result in a complete loss of the intangible, or change in the tradition of rituals of performance and ceremony (Fontein 2006). Archaeological evidence fits into the category of tangible material remains (Kirshenblatt-Gimblett 2004) and very often these are prioritized at the expense of the intangible. The critique levelled against colonial archaeology aptly captures some of the limitations of archaeology as a discipline, which, until recently has failed to engage fairly with descendant communities.

It was also noted at the Victoria Falls meeting that there are cases where conservation practices at sites seem to be in conflict with intangible values. The conservation programmes archaeologists and heritage managers conduct on the stonewalled heritage in Zimbabwe is an apt example (Ndoro 2004; Ndoro and Pwiti 2001; Ndoro and Chirikure 2009). This is generally at odds with communities who perceive the ruinous nature of such sites as something that is in keeping with such places' spiritual values. Minimal upkeep of such places would be in tandem with their intangible values, as continuity of intangible cultural values requires tangible manifestation and the identity of the past and present closely linked in many instances with intangible dimensions. The same applies to burials, which are sacred places, but which archaeologists have been interfering with. Current and past approaches and interpretations in archaeology require re-examining to unravel some of the apparent anomalies between sites and their functions and re-establish the vital connections between the tangible and intangible. I use this argument to suggest that current archaeological perception and definition of 'site' must be reconsidered.

6.4.3 *Under the Colonial Shade*

A graphic account for the disrespect of the dead comes from the activities of Theodore Bent (1969), the first antiquarian to excavate at Great Zimbabwe, who at the same time had fascinating encounters with communities living within the precincts of the settlement. I am fascinated by his treatment of burials found during his excavations of the site in 1891:

> In our work at [Great] Zimbabwe we unwittingly opened several of their graves amongst the old ruins. The corpse had been laid out on a reed mat – the mat, probably, on which he had slept during life. His bowl and his calabash were placed beside him. One of these graves had been made in a narrow passage in the ancient walls on the fortress. We were rather horrified at what we had done, especially as a man came to complain, and said that it was the grave of his brother, who had died a year before; so we filled up the aperture and resisted the temptation to proceed with our excavations at that spot. After that the old chief Ikomo, whenever we started a fresh place, came and told us a relation of his was buried there. This occurring so often, we began to suspect, and eventually proved, a fraud. So we set sentiment aside and took scientific research as our motto for the future. (Bent 1969, 79).

The recklessness around the pillaging of Great Zimbabwe by antiquarian investigators may be the reason why there is no information on human remains from this site, but at the same time this experience graphically illustrates the colonial disregard of indigenous cultural values pertaining to the dead. The attitude displayed by Bent and his team, while apologetic about disturbing what could have been fresh burials at Great Zimbabwe at the time he conducted his research, also implied that the local, African clans had nothing to do with the construction of Great Zimbabwe. Once they proved that the local claims about the burials were a 'fraud', they disregarded their sentiments and embarked on what they defined as 'scientific research'. Bent's (1969) projection of archaeology as a science whose findings were far more important ahead of community values underlines a persistent attitude among some scholars today. The insensitivity to which certain research was conducted deeply annoyed indigenous communities. Here is another experience Theodore Bent had at Great Zimbabwe:

> One day as we were digging in a cave we came across the skeleton of a goat tied on to a mat with bark string; by its side was the carved knife, with portions of the goat's hair still adhering to it. Here we had an obvious instance of sacrifice, a sacrifice which takes place, I believe, to avert calamity— famine, war, or pestilence— which at the time threatens the community. The natives were very reticent on the point, but visibly annoyed at our discovery (Bent 1969, 79–80).

However, Bent must be credited for giving himself time to study 'native' cultural beliefs, and although very cynical in his remarks, he acknowledges one important link between the living and the dead; that the Karanga people are "great believers in making themselves agreeable to the departed" (Bent 1969, 79). This observation is replete in 20th century ethnographic accounts, a subject to which I now turn.

6.4.4 *Shona Worldview and Connections between the Living and the Dead*

To illustrate the importance of reburial in the context of cultural heritage conservation, I discuss the worldview of the Shona people— whose ancestors are believed to be the founders of the civilisations of Mapungubwe and Great Zimbabwe (Huffman 1996; Pikirayi 2001). Venda people partly derive from the Shona (Beach 1980) and claim cultural connections with Mapungubwe (Ralushai 2005). The Shona people live within the boundaries of modern Zimbabwe, although some live in adjacent Botswana, Mozambique and South Africa. For the definition of the Shona, I accept Holleman's (1952) critique that this term is an identity attributed from outside, and that the 'dialectical clusters' of Zezuru, Korekore, Karanga, Kalanga and Manyika are superficial, for people who share the same language, the same worldview, and broadly, the same environment. Although there is considerable local and regional variation in their cultural practices, the processes regarding the rituals and ceremonies around rainmaking, agriculture, marriage, death, etc., are broadly similar (Edwards 1928).

The Shona have an extensive settlement system, the smallest unit being the homestead (*mana*), followed by the village (*musha*), then ward (*dunhu*) and finally region or country (*nyika*) (Holleman 1952 and 1953). Authority is vested in the family elder, the hereditary headman at the village level, the ward head and the chief at country level. This quasi hierarchical structure also reflects socio-economic organisation (Holleman 1952; Weinrich 1971). Social composition becomes less homogenous from the ward level upwards, and the size of the country (Holleman 1961, 372), some 30–90 kilometres across, approximately corresponds with chiefdom-level political organisation (Pikirayi 1993, 188). Country corresponds to the widest grouping functioning as a political and territorial unit. In the *nyika* are *vatorwa*, the majority of the population, who owe their allegiance to the chief and his lineage, *machinda*. These belong to a number of other lineages. The bulk of the *vatorwa* usually come into the territory in search for land or political safety or as individual families eager to settle with or near their maternal or uterine relatives (Holleman 1952, 16).

As homesteads and villages grow, they also define a new world around them; that of the dead. Death is part of Shona life and is always accompanied by ritual and ceremony. In most cases, the dead are buried close to the homestead or selected areas owned by the family, which could be a cave or cleft within a rocky outcrop, or the soft dumb soil by the river or near a termite heap. In some cases, this could be a couple of kilometres from the homestead (Bourdillon 1987, 233–34). The dead body is buried facing the direction of lineage origin and the grave is marked with personal possessions (Kuper, Hughes and Veslen 1954, 37; Bullock 1927). Graves or burials should never be tempered with in any way, as the dead must rest in peace (Pwiti 1996a). Funerals are accompanied by rites and ceremonies, but this does not end with burial of the deceased. For married men and women, with children especially sons, concluding ceremonies are conducted a year or two after death. These ceremonies are conducted over and around the grave, where matters of inheritance are settled. Continuity between the living and the dead is ritually sanctioned by anointing an heir, who is given the personal name of the deceased and by allotting widows to the deceased's kinsman (Posselt 1935; Kuper, Hughes and Veslen 1954, 33). If the deceased is a married woman, the surviving spouse may remarry, but this has to be sanctioned by elders of the family as well as the father of the widow.

The world of the dead belongs to the *vadzimu* [singular *mudzimu*], which are family spirits of mature or elderly dead parents, men and women and grandparents, and not normally unmarried men or women. These spirits are normally protective of the living (Gelfand 1962, 51) regardless of whether they have relocated elsewhere or not, and reside permanently around the homesteads or village, whether abandoned or not. Thus they are sometimes regarded as guardian spirits or spirit elders, something which implies that the dead are also 'living' (Richards 1942). These spirits are venerated, and this may be directed to either a single or plurality of ancestors (Bullock 1950, 130). Since ancestral spirits represent continuity of the family line, they may be retributive if their living descendants forget them, or if a ritual or ceremony is omitted or improperly conducted, or if one breaks the law, or if they find themselves in a situation where they have no one to convey their wants or talk to. The Shona believe this may be carrying a punishment of serious illness or death.

According to Posselt (1927, 1930, and 1935, 89–90), the power of the dead varies with the status they had in life. Chiefs received distinctive burial. Their bodies were adorned with animal skins, e.g., that of a bull, and preserved through sealing and drying, before being interred in a secret cave or a cleft enclosed with granite stones or slabs. The spirit of chiefs wielded greatest power and received most elaborate recognition. This took place annually, according to Theodore Bent (1969), reporting on the Makaranga around Great Zimbabwe in the early 1890s: "In the tomb of a chief, it is customary to place a bowl of beer, which is constantly replenished for the refreshment of the spirit...and the annual sacrificial feast in honour of the dead meat and beer are always allotted to the spirits of their ancestors" (p. 79).

In this regard, some ancestral or spirit elders assume a regional significance. According to Gelfand (1962, 51), these *mhondoro*, or spirits that come out from a burial and transform themselves into maneless lions (1935, 24) protect an ethnic group, and derive from the founder of the clan (*rudzi*).

There is a link between the chief, every member of the ethnic group and the regional spirit protecting it. Chiefs are often buried together in a remote spot from any habitation and taboo to all except on ritual occasions (Bourdillon 1987, 234). For the Manyika people of eastern Zimbabwe, the mountain of Bingaguru is often connected with this (Bhila 1982). In other parts of the Shona world, the chiefs were buried in cave tunnels known as *ninga* or *nhare*, on prominent hills or mountains. Such landscapes are therefore 'owned' by the lineage of the chief, and may not be used by other lineages. According to Kuper, Huges and van Veslen (1954), each *nyika* has a hill refuge (*nhare*) which is regarded as the ancestral burial place of chiefs and the place of sacrifice to the lineage spirits (Bullock 1950, 202).

Thus through spirit elders, the tangible world of the living, is protected, and to a greater extent, reliant upon the world of the dead. It is critical that these spirits are not forgotten by the living, lest they are punished through witchcraft or illness. This may be reserved through propiation and other sacrificial offerings, where a beast is dedicated. Death should not be the cause of homestead of village abandonment. Disease, strange illnesses, disasters like flooding or droughts may drive this process in extreme cases. Normally, abandoned settlements (*matongo*; singular, *dongo*) are primarily a consequence of population growth, with parent houses splitting up into component smaller units. According to Holleman (1953), abandonment was also conditioned by failure by a number of homesteads (*dzimba*) and villages (*misha*) to attain political and territorial autonomy. In other cases, it was conditioned by ritual. Abandonment did not imply complete desertion of settlements, or that people gave up their claims and interests to a place (see critique in Colwell-Chanthaphonh and Ferguson 2006, 37). Human-land relationships implied that this interest be maintained in perpetuity.

Because of the importance of spirit elders (*midzimu*), some sites may have been abandoned but in fact continue to be used in the present— in a spiritual sense, such as the case of Great Zimbabwe (Fontein 2006). On the contrary, the way archaeologists have often perceived Great Zimbabwe is conditioned by the reading of behavioural archaeology, which, according to Colwell-Chanthaphonh and Ferguson (2006, 38) structures elements as either a systemic context or an archaeological context. This is a dichotomy which leads researchers to see objects or artefacts as refuse and sites as abandoned. However, it is difficult to perceive a site or a region as abandoned when the people once living there show continuous connections with such places. Archaeologists generally focus on the "mystery of leaving" and not enough attention on many ways that connections to homelands are maintained (Colwell-Chanthaphonh and Ferguson 2006, 38). The Karanga, for example, did not in effect completely abandon Great Zimbabwe, but maintained connections with the site and the landscape over centuries, as 17th century movements to the south suggest (Beach 1980 and 1994).

This analysis is not new knowledge, but simply a selection of relevant ethnographic data collected since the early 20th century that serves to understand the context in which human remains must be reburied where they have been excavated. These ethnographic data were mainly for colonial administrators, which archaeologists had access to. It is unfortunate that this data was not used to inform archaeological approaches or practice. The archaeology of human burials has gone largely unnoticed in many parts of southern Africa as Africans lost their land to Europeans. The sacred nature of these and associated landscapes (see Edwards 1928) were lost as European rule made it difficult for indigenous people to scrutinise the actions of archaeologists, while claims for land lost to white commercial farming were not entertained. This was to result in scholarship that was highly quantitative traditional archaeology— a science with practically no relevance to the general public or specifically, to communities where such research was carried out.

6.4.5 *Implications for Cultural Heritage*

Burial archaeology in southern Africa largely relates to cultural developments of the last two millennia. This period is synonymous with development of agro-pastoral and complex social formations synonymous with state societies such as Mapungubwe, Great Zimbabwe, Khami and later kingdoms. While pottery is the primary evidence used, some associated data exists in the form of human skeletal remains found in burials and associated settlements (see Mitchell 2002; Sutton 1994–1995). What is glaringly missing in the archaeological reports is relevant ethnography (Ucko 1969), resulting in dry, uninformative interpretations of the past. There is a mismatch between the archaeological evidence and the ethnography, which have stifled relevant archaeological interpretation (see Pwiti and Mahachi 1991). Archaeologists either recover settlements or burials, rarely both at the same time. What archaeologists regard as archaeology of ritual is that which is associated with death and funerary processes and not residences. This approach characterised burial archaeology in Zimbabwe and adjacent countries, in both colonial and postcolonial contexts, where burial sites were treated differently from settlements. Archaeological sites of the Harare and Musengezi traditions (12th to 16th centuries AD) in central and northern Zimbabwe were thought of essentially as funerary in character, until archaeologists uncovered associated settlements (Marufu 2008: Pikirayi 1987: Pwiti 1996b).

The reason why the Karanga and the Venda attach so much importance to the dead is that death is a considerable process subsuming a number of rituals and ceremonies commencing well before death and ending a year or two after the burial (Gelfand 1962, 120–35). The ceremonies of *mharadzano* (parting with the deceased) and *kurova guva* (a special ceremony to welcome 'back home' the spirit of the deceased) serve to institute certain members of the family as ancestors. These post-death rituals and ceremonies connect the living with the ancestral world. They do not exhume bodies in graves for reburial elsewhere. These are left intact, as exhumation entails disturbing the spirit. If need arises to bring the dead person 'back home', a soil sample from around the grave is taken and then reburied at the new location to symbolize the spiritual presence of that person. This also means that a settlement can never be completely abandoned since the burials nearby retain the spiritual attachment to a residential site. This makes it possible to return to such a place and re-settle. This is in tandem with spiritual reconnection referred to earlier in this work. In this context, residential sites do not lose their sacred connections with the dead even if there is no known direct link with living or historically known ethnographic communities. This is what colonial archaeologists missed in their approaches to burial archaeology in southern Africa. Antiquarians and early archaeologists received the protection of colonial administrators enabling them to work on African lands without consent from local or descendant communities. The appropriation of African land into European farmland or wildlife parks or sanctuaries further cushioned the profession of archaeology as sites were investigated without taking into account the intangible significance of such places. Communities had effectively lost touch with their original *matongo* and were not able to return to reclaim them or pay heed to the graves of their dead as, according to the ethnography, is required by tradition.

6.5 Why Protect Archaeological Heritage?

Recent discussions on cultural heritage show a growing concern with archaeological heritage and cultural property increasingly becoming targets of high priority in armed conflicts and the "cultural cleansing" of whole regions becoming one of the prime goals of warfare. This has become the context and the incentive for the looting and destruction of archaeological sites as well as religious buildings and cultural institutions, such as libraries, archives, and museums (Schipper and Bernhardsson 2010). This targeting, looting and destruction of cultural property connected to armed conflicts threatens scientific investigation on, conservation of, and general access to cultural heritage. This may not be of immediate concern to South Africa and its neighbours, but Schipper and Bernhardsson (2010) point out that this has to do with people's identities: "The protection of cultural heritage is not merely about monuments and artefacts but about people and identity. Consequently, preserving cultural heritage is not about the past but concerns the present and future of humankind."

Which identities and values are heritage professionals protecting in the research area? In any site management plan, we are not just protecting the tangible cultural and other remains, but the values in which these remains stand for. UNESCO inscribed the site on the list on the basis of criteria (ii), (iii), (iv) and (v). Its landscape contains evidence for an important interchange of human values that resulted in significant cultural and social changes in the southern African region between AD 900 and 1300. The landscape has archaeological evidence attesting to the existence of a state society, which at the time was the largest in the region. This state had trading connections with eastern Africa and Asia, attesting to the exchange of human values. Scientists have also documented evidence of climate change in the area, which archaeologists have used to model the growth and demise of the kingdom based on and around Mapungubwe hill. This kingdom therefore attests to a culture that became vulnerable to irreversible change.

The simplest idea behind condition assessments at sites chosen for study was to produce measured surveys and other baseline data critical for cultural heritage conservation. Such records, which describe in sufficient detail the physical and dimensional configuration of a heritage at a given point in time, may become invaluable in future. But the nature of current heritage protection the world over is too professional-*centric*. This is evident in some of the Getty conservation manuals, where one of the guiding principles on who should conduct heritage information activities clearly states: "Heritage information activities should be carried out first and foremost by professionals; however, everyone with an interest in the heritage place and who has information to contribute should also participate" (Letellier 2007, xvii).

6.6 Conclusion

The interpretations presented in this chapter try to address some of the research questions raised earlier. The present scenario visibly explains why there are community barriers to access, interaction, use and negotiation with the past as far as cultural heritage places are concerned.

Apart from the human-land relationships, the new management authorities for sites and cultural landscapes, descendant communities are not residential. In trying to situate the Mapungubwe re-burials in the context of heritage conservation, I used Shona instead of Venda ethnography, although the latter are claimants to the site and associated landscape. This is problematic in that current configurations of political boundaries situate Mapungubwe firmly in South Africa, making it a South African heritage place, largely inaccessible by claimants, if any, from neighbouring countries. However, this does not negate the need to employ Venda ethnography in understanding how (re)burials signify the sacredness and importance of heritage places, which must be protected or conserved.

The meaning of conservation in a 'traditional' context is totally different from that used and perceived in professional circles. Archaeologists and heritage managers claim authenticity and other tangible 'visibles' on a site and cultural landscape and in doing so, follow a set of prescribed rules and guidelines. Descendant communities preserve sites quite differently. In preservation it is not the rebuilding or reconstruction that matters (Meskell 2007), but the acknowledgement of cultural heritage values (Manyanga, pers. com). Even the ruinous nature of some sites may serve to underline the presence of some of the values that we should acknowledge. The connection is mainly through the intangible as communities who acknowledge spiritual values of such places imbue it with cultural significance (see Gonçalves et al. 2003). It is through the intangible component that communities locate their own pasts in cultural heritage places such as archaeological sites.

Little consideration has been given for reburial of the human remains as an exercise in conserving cultural heritage. The experience with the reburial demonstrates that you may not conserve a site when there is nothing to conserve. Thus the stabilization exercise at Mapungubwe, Bambandyanalo and Schroda (Nienaber and Hutten 2006), while well framed within the context of protection of archaeological remains of world heritage proportions and developed as part of an exercise in assisting nearby communities in terms of employment (Pikirayi 2011), did not carry much cultural relevance to descendant communities.

In these wide ranging interpretations of cultural heritage, it is clear that the past is always changing our lives and that its role is constantly shifting. According to Lowenthal (1985), heritage can sometimes be nurturing and sometimes burdensome, but always challenging us to understand the present whilst imposing powerful constraints upon the way that present develops. This is the reason why some aspects of the past are celebrated, while others are deleted from public memory or conveniently sidelined. Each generation, he argues, reshapes its legacy in line with current needs.

Some of the legacies are shaped by opportunistic developments such as the discovery of coal in an area just adjacent to the buffer zone of the

Mapungubwe Cultural Landscape and World Heritage site. This resulted in interested and affected parties raising concerns and objections to the proposed mining developments. The developments would include prospecting on the farm Machete, an open-cast mine, and the construction of a power station, all adjacent to the World Heritage site. Some archaeologists, environmentalists and civic groups mounted spirited opposition to these proposed developments, arguing that they would destroy archaeological resources, the fragile environment of the area and compromise the integrity of the World Heritage site. The affected parties called for a thorough public consultations process. Due to time constraints and since this matter took centre stage when this project was nearing completion, I can only make brief comments here. Concerns mainly from the archaeological community in South Africa suggest that the state of archaeology had not reached a point where it may be regarded as community-based. In arguing against development, no consideration was made on the role of archaeology among descendant communities, who are mostly poor and who could benefit from the mining or other forms of environmental exploitation in the area. This raises the question whether archaeology can be really in the service of humanity, presented with the challenges of economic recession, unemployment, poverty, and the ever-increasing gap between the rich and the poor in South Africa. Can archaeology be of relevance in contemporary South Africa if it serves apparently parochial interests? The final chapter discusses the issue of relevance in the broader context of sharing the past between archaeologists and descendant communities.

CHAPTER SEVEN

Conclusions and Recommendations: Archaeology, the Public and the Future

7.1 Introduction

The research questions and problems highlighted in this study are now discussed in broader global context and issues of relevance are raised. The first research question raised in the study focused on how communities and the public in the research area accessed, interacted and used some of the sites, and/or negotiated with the past *in the present*. A corollary to this question involved understanding the nature and form of barriers to access, interaction, use and negotiation with the past as experienced by descent communities in the research area. The second research question centred on community perception of what professionals refer to as conservation of cultural and even natural heritage, and whether this understanding was in agreement with what 'tradition' prescribes. An alternative way of looking at this research question was probing how local and descend communities locate their own pasts in cultural heritage places such as archaeological sites. The third research question focused on archaeology in relation to modern development challenges. Given recent developments in the research area connected with repatriation and restitution, and the further granting of a license to a mining company to exploit an area adjacent to a world heritage cultural landscape, and the reactions of archaeologists, environmentalists, stakeholders and other interested persons, the question is whether southern Africa is moving towards community-based archaeology or whether archaeology is still a largely 'reactive' or 'legislative-compliant', academic discipline. Can archaeology be really in the service of humanity, presented with the challenges of unemployment, poverty, etc?

A recent discussion convened by Little (2009) raised the issue of archaeological relevance in the present. Entitled "What Can Archaeology Do for Justice, Peace, Community, and the Earth?", the forum contributed to the ongoing conversation about archaeology as it might be of service beyond its traditional roles. The forum observed that archaeology has always played a role in society beyond its contribution to knowledge and that there are increasing numbers of archaeologists determined to use their expertise to make the world a better place. The need to take a long-term view of the past— in this context 'tradition' to inform the present and future— situates archaeology centrally to the discussion and some of the recommendations presented in this chapter. I do not pretend that this work is a policy document meant to advise decision makers in heritage circles on what course of action to take for archaeology to reclaim its position in contemporary society. It is essentially a critique, and ultimately, a dissatisfaction with archaeology as practiced in the present. My focus is on archaeology helping in building communities, promoting heritage and identity, and, in the process, recognising the value of the *long duree* – tradition. The key terms here are relevance and engagement.

7.2 Archaeology beyond Disciplinary Boundaries

'Archaeology has become a means whereby people from many cultural backgrounds can participate in and discuss issues of mutual interest, local or global' (Cunliffe, Gosden and Joyce 2009, xiii).

In his 2004 book *Archaeology and Ancient History: Breaking Down the Boundaries,* Eberhard Sauer argues that the divide between archaeology and history has long been problematical and there seems little chance of resolution in the near future. It is, however, evident that even within the wider discipline of archaeology, there are divisions within the academic study of the past and numerous suggestions have been offered to narrow this divide, including multidisciplinary approaches to the study and understanding of the past. This sharing of the past by archaeologists, although it has gone a long way in disentangling the complex nature of the discipline, has, however, failed to define either the role archaeology should play in history or its broader relevance to society. In southern Africa, archaeologists still struggle to make their work relevant to a variety of communities and the general public. The main problem is the esoteric nature of the discipline and the power of the artefact in the production of archaeological knowledge. This is further distanced from the communities and the broader public where archaeologists are confronted with issues such as environmental conservation and sustainability, land claims, economic development, heritage and identity, racism and so on. Thus the relevance of archaeology lies not only in what archaeologists do by themselves in order to understand the past, but also in what they achieve in the company of non-archaeologists, including interacting and engaging with communities.

This concluding chapter provides an assessment of how archaeologists deal with community engagement in southern Africa, showing, among other things, that engaging the public can address and reshape the structure of communication with descendant communities, and experts from other disciplines. As demonstrated in some of the papers presented at the Sixth World Archaeological Congress (WAC) in Dublin in June-July 2008, this exercise has potential to recast the roles and responsibilities of archaeologists to the communities in and with which they work. Community engagement enables archaeologists to recognise the voices of the communities and other stakeholders, ensuring that these become active participants in the course of the archaeological process. Such 'engaged archaeologies' are also regarded as useful archaeologies that provide relevant and timely information which serves as a tool for solving social and scientific problems, thus making archaeology an integral part of the broader heritage discourse.

The research has highlighted issues pertaining to archaeologists' experience of community engagement in the Limpopo Province of South Africa, the concept of community involvement in archaeology, the power relations underpinning community involvement, and, how the past, in this context represented by the archaeological heritage, is negotiated and contested between various communities. It can be concluded that conservation of some archaeological sites is best achieved by integrating 'scientific knowledge' with community-held knowledge of these places. Community-held knowledge, which is acquired through a process of engaged and collaborative conversation and dialogue with communities, provides information to archaeologists and heritage managers for use on the conservation of sites and monuments. I perceive this sharing of archaeological and related information that situates the archaeologist as the learner, instead of that long perceived 'expert' who 'tells' communities what to do. It is this latter practice which continues to alienate archaeology from communities that it seeks to study.

This chapter looks at archaeology in two ways: firstly, how archaeologists can disentangle the highly academic nature of archaeology and make it more relevant to non-archaeologists and, secondly, how archaeologists should actively engage descendant communities in their quest to understand and protect the past. I borrow from Joe Watkins (2005) the phrase 'wary eyes' not only to make references to wide-ranging discussion on indigenous peoples all over the world and their changing perceptions of archaeology and relations with archaeologists, but also to invoke a continuous concern among archaeologists in terms of how they share knowledge given the nature of the discipline and its relationship with others. Besides, the relevance of archaeology as a discipline is continuously questioned and debated (Little 2009).

The chapter recommends mechanisms for sharing knowledge, methods and approaches between archaeologists and heritage practitioners in southern Africa tasked with the teaching and conservation of sites and collections, on the one hand, and the public, specifically relevant communities, on the other. The objective is to offer opportunities for reviewing, discussing and comparing living approaches or limitations in the sharing of archaeological knowledge within the colonial, apartheid and postcolonial or post-apartheid context in which the discipline is now situated.

Recent studies have shown that the relationship between archaeology and the public or community continues to change (Marshall 2002 and 2009). The public are increasingly showing an interest in the past, its presentation and representation, and interpretation. Some are actively participating in the drawing up of archaeological research projects and participating in the excavation of sites (Pikirayi 2007). It is this relationship with the public which calls for a transformed archaeology, particularly in countries where the discipline was introduced as part of the

European colonial enterprise, and alienated the heritage of local peoples. More specifically, in South Africa, there is discussion on the role a transformed archaeology should play in a once racially divided multicultural society. In this context, archaeologists need to redefine the future role of the discipline and how the general public as well as specific communities can increasingly access and make use of archaeological data.

7.3 Making Archaeology Useful: The Quest for Relevance through Engagement

The theme 'Engaged and Useful Archaeologies' convened at the Sixth World Archaeological Congress identified ecological conservation and sustainability, land claims, economic development, promotion of heritage and identity, community building, and fighting racism, among others, as topical issues where archaeologists could apply their work to non-archaeologists. The theme also accepted other ways of knowing the past, especially ancient traditions. Pitted against problems such as war, racism, starvation, famine, poverty, and environmental degradation, can archaeology resolve or address these problems? One scholar has suggested that archaeologists need to restructure or re-shape or communicate with communities of aboriginal people and researchers from other disciplines (Little 2009). Such engaged archaeologies have the potential to recast the roles and responsibilities of archaeologists to communities in and with which they work (Gadsby *et al.* 2008, 158). Such archaeologies recognise the voices of indigenous groups, descendant communities and other constituencies, empowering them in the entire archaeological process. They also provide relevant, useful and timely information which can serve as a tool for solving social and scientific problems. When treated in this way, Gadsby *et al.* (2008) argued, engaged and useful archaeologies become an effective foil for intellectual colonialism, casting researchers as facilitators who have something to offer in exchange for archaeological data, and help to balance the complex power relationships between researchers and communities.

When archaeology is shared with the public in the manner described here, Gadsby *et al.* (2008) believe it becomes a tool for civic engagement, activism and social justice, and a powerful source of information about human origins. But how do the public and communities view archaeology in Africa in general and southern Africa in particular? Archaeology is perceived as a discipline which exploits the past, including the dead (Scheoman and Pikirayi 2008). According to Watkins (2005), archaeology is viewed by indigenous peoples as a colonialist enterprise with continuing political undertones (2005, 433), and this attitude has to change. In southern Africa, archaeology that simply seeks to recover a lost and distant past, as is largely the case, has no appeal among aboriginal or indigenous communities. Such archaeology is for academic purposes, and in most cases, is peripheral or irrelevant to communities. These communities prefer an archaeology that presents them an opportunity to engage with the past in a beneficial way— a challenge to the essence of archaeology perceived in academia as a 'science' of recovering the past. The quest for relevance is not difficult to attain as archaeology has generated useful data, for example, long- and short-term past environmental data can be used to engage with climate change and social responses to such changes. Such data needs to be communicated to communities in much the same way as seismologists would communicate effects of earthquakes and volcanic eruptions to those closely affected. And also because of the ever-changing environment, it is necessary to continuously revisit current archaeological heritage management and conservation approaches.

The discussion here goes beyond the definitions of, and approaches to, community archaeology as presented elsewhere Marshall (2002) and in the southern African region by Chirikure and Pwiti (2008), Fontein (2006), Ndoro (2001), and others. Here, I argue that sharing the past with non-archaeologists is an exercise that transforms the nature of the discipline in a profound way. I now illustrate this point, demonstrating that archaeology needs to correct its imperialist, nationalist or colonial focus by listening to other voices which underline the deep concerns the public and communities have about archaeologists.

7.4 The Relevance of Archaeology in Southern Africa

How archaeology relates to indigenous or local communities, however defined, remains critical the world over—the main problem being archaeologists' treatment of cultural treasures including human remains found in or among those communities. It is ironic that even here in southern Africa, South Africa in particular, archaeologists have failed to articulate the relevance of their own discipline to society, despite the region being replete with evidence for humanity's origins, and historical dynamics of social identities formed during the past half millennia. Archaeology still carries a bad image, often associated with desecration of sacred places including burials. To the majority of southern Africans, its usefulness is limited to knowledge production which only benefits archaeologists. Government authorities are distrustful of archaeologists, whose demographics are embarrassingly skewed towards the white minority. To many, archaeology in a postcolonial context is firmly grounded in a 'buried' as well as bitter past, including slavery, European colonialism, apartheid, land alienation, and other painful pasts. The conflict arising from exhumation of human remains in Prestwich Street, Cape Town, illustrates this perception quite vividly (Shepherd 2007).

If the Prestwich Street experience represented archaeologists distancing themselves from society and culture, and leaving communities bitter, the December 2007 reburial of human remains excavated since the 1930s from the Mapungubwe Cultural Landscape brought about a sense of community building and interaction with archaeologists. This was not easy though, given the quarrels between the claimant groups, who tried to authenticate their claims by proving sole ownership of the remains. In this potentially volatile context, archaeologists were not just negotiating responsible repatriation; they were also considering their role in a racially and ethnically divided present (Schoeman and Pikirayi 2011). This would fit into Barbara Little's integrative approach, where the interests of science (archaeology) have to take into account those of society (humanities). Archaeologists need to go beyond this by situating their discipline within community needs and expectations. Communities must set parameters for relevant archaeologies, and their voices must be heard (see Fontein 2006).

'Engaging Archaeologies' was one of the themes of 2008's World Archaeological Congress (WAC) in Dublin. The basis for such archaeologies lies in the advocacy for community participation in the management of archaeological and other cultural heritage. Dating from the mid 1990s, such calls did not clearly define the term 'community,' and how such participation could be achieved. Engaged archaeologies should adopt pluralistic approaches to the study of the past, as communities have rejected archaeologists' narratives of their pasts, often based on interpretations of 'layered' evidence or selected parts of sites such as garbage mounds.

The benefits of archaeology in southern Africa, particularly Zimbabwe— arguably the only country in the world named after an archaeological site—should be self-evident, given its highly politicised heritage, including land restitution. Zimbabwe's archaeological past may be made to look relevant in the present, even if we do not understand what some of this past is, or represents (Pikirayi 2006). Communities still make use of such pasts, though. Such 'usable pasts' are a necessary public empowering tool, where those in positions of control often manipulate the public in order to project their own views of the world. In Zimbabwe, such usable pasts are driven by historical and cultural experiences such as losses experienced by communities due to European colonisation, land alienation, racial segregation, and other injustices, much of which are fixed in people's memories (see Holtorf 1996). Other pasts appeal to those in the present in so many ways. In Zimbabwe, Mozambique and South Africa, Great Zimbabwe-style monumental architecture is used to re-create or remember the pre-European past (see Riegl 1996). Great Zimbabwe, Khami, Mapungubwe, and other 'monuments' symbolise a culturally rich past before European colonisation and domination. Some of the injustices of colonialism can apparently be addressed by appealing to the pre-European past as represented by these sites and places.

In articulating the relevance of archaeology, the global justice movement could not have come at a better time. The destruction of the treasures of Iraq reflected how war and those in corridors of power could violate other people's cultural heritage with impunity, all in the name of human rights and democracy, while in essence pursuing parochial national and international self-interests. I am familiar with the principles of the University of Sheffield-based Archaeology for Global Justice (AGJ), through ARCH-JUSTICE, their WAC mailing list. I see them seeking to redraw or redefine the principles of archaeological practice in the post-modern world characterised by much social injustice, discrimination, social inequality, differential access to resources, poverty, violence, environmental degradation and unsustainable development. Besides, by seeking to engage the public and re-establishing professionalism based on equality and open debate, they are advocating the kind of archaeology that southern Africa should do in a postcolonial or post-apartheid environment. While this may be seen as a way of redressing past cultural injustices committed in a violent world of European colonialism and apartheid, archaeology may address relevance in other interesting ways beyond the confines of justice. If Zimbabwean archaeologists were to team up with political scientists to probe decline or collapse in modernity and its connections, if any, with pre-colonial social formations, more answers may be found as to why we attach so much importance to Great Zimbabwe (AD 1280–1550) and associated cultural heritage.

To close this section, I address relevance beyond communities. Relevance here is contextualised within a developing world perspective, and thus different from Western Europe and the United States. For argument sake, how can archaeology be in the service of United Nations Millennium Development Goals (MDGs)? This is where we must benchmark what society regards as relevant to their needs, and how our discipline should situate itself to address concerns of a global nature. The UN has identified and defined eight goals: eradication of extreme poverty and hunger; achieving universal primary education; promoting gender equity and empowering women; reducing child mortality; improving maternal health; combating HIV/AIDS, malaria and other diseases; ensuring environmental sustainability; and, developing a global partnership for development (http://www.un.org/millenniumgoals). These goals as outlined must be achieved by 2015! However, the goals sideline culture as a vehicle for development. A study by Pro Helvetia and the Swiss Agency for Development and Cooperation (SDC) in seven Eastern European countries reveals that cultural work plays a key role in the social development of transition countries (Landry 2006). According to the study, cultural work strengthens diversity of opinion and promotes debate on socially relevant topics. It also helps to create alternative structures and networks and facilitates participation in political life. Cultural work also reinforces civil society, particularly in emerging and fragile democracies. It is unfortunate that when such agendas are being conceptualized, archaeologists are nowhere to be found!

7.5 How Sharing Enhances the Protection of Archaeological Heritage

It has been demonstrated elsewhere in the world that archaeology can create a useful partnership between archaeologists, the public and local communities who constitute an important knowledge base (Marshall 2009, 202). How archaeologists process such knowledge and communicate it beyond the confines of their disciplinary precincts should redefine the nature and character of archaeology in post-colonial southern Africa. Archaeological heritage protection can effectively be achieved if done in close partnership with the public and local communities (Chirikure and Pwiti 2008; Fontein 2006). Although southern Africa has taken advanced strides in archaeological conservation (see Ndoro 2001), the discipline needs to share its goals and achievements to the public and communities. The current study was conceived out of the desire to disentangle archaeology from its highly academic nature and make it more relevant to non-archaeologists and, secondly, to actively engage archaeologists with descendant communities in their quest to conserve the archaeological heritage using community-based knowledge and resources (see Raphael and Quan 2002).

This research has been motivated by current developments in the research area that include the reburial of human remains at the archaeological site of Thulamela in the Kruger National Park (Meskell 2007); the inscription of the archaeological sites of Mapungubwe and Bambandyanalo on the World Heritage List; and the stabilisation programmes embarked upon by the South African National Parks (SANPaks) on these sites to save archaeological deposits (Nienaber and Hutten 2006) as part of a broader conviction that the postcolonial or post-apartheid era would bring an end to the destruction of archaeological heritage. These developments have implications for archaeological conservation and what it means to the people who claim these places. They must be placed within a much broader debate on whether we should resort to the 'Old School' (Maradze 2004) in cultural heritage conservation; pre-colonial forms of management of such places (Ndoro 2001), the potential conflicts arising from community contestations as they demand increased access to such places (Fontein 2006; Msemwa 2005; Stewart, Clark and Fulford 2004). It is still unclear whether southern Africa is moving towards community-based archaeology or simply 'reactive' or 'consent-based' community involvement (see for example Greer, Harrison, and McIntyre-Tamwoy 2002) or community-based participatory research (see Atalay 2007). Perhaps the latter is more often the case, given current legislative framework governing cultural (including archaeological) heritage, which places further constraint towards access of communities to archaeological heritage. Thus, it is appropriate to talk about engaged archaeologies, a term which bridges conventional archaeology with what others refer to as indigenous archaeology (Atalay 2007).

Preliminary results also indicate that in applying modern conservation approaches to these places, we often ignore community knowledge about how these places were 'abandoned' and the cultural meaning of such leaving processes in terms of site conservation. Archaeologists obliterate a range of human behaviours, often reducing complex processes to simple or non-events. While communities did abandon such places in the past, oral information tells us that human-land relationships implied that they did not give up claims to places they had settled originally. This is demonstrated by continued use of some of these sites in the present.

A topic that this research did not cover is traditional legislation pertaining to the protection of cultural heritage places and landscapes. This is important in preserving the integrity of heritage and in ensuring that heritage is more efficiently managed. In a landscape which has witnessed considerable transformation and historical layering, the impact of change on tradition requires constant review. Traditional legislation is beginning to receive considerable attention in much of the African continent as it is an inseparable aspect of heritage conservation (Ndoro 2008; Ndoro, Mumma and Abungu 2008; Ndoro and Pwiti 2005).

The world is increasingly adopting non-Western views of heritage, and this has a major impact on cultural heritage preservation. According to Raphael and Quan (2002), the non-Western view includes 'non-rational' factors perceiving heritage objects as part of a universe that is energised and animated by forms of divine and supernatural power. It puts less emphasis on original construction fabric and accepts traditional restorations. It works to preserve the social value of heritage and equally to protect intangible values. This is in sharp contrast to Western preservation strategies, which perceive science, secularisation and modernisation as the future. In doing so, they marginalise living religious practices and current usage; lack the involvement of aboriginal people in the conservation and management of their heritage; focus on 'material integrity' and 'original fabric', ignoring social context, intangible values and roles; and, do not truly respect supernatural belief systems, viewing them as 'superstitious' and primitive.

7.6 Conclusion

Sharing archaeology among archaeologists, between archaeologists and non-archaeologists, and for purposes of enhancing the protection of archaeological heritage is an exercise in engaging with issues of the past and the roles they play in the present. Archaeology should no longer be regarded as the science of generating knowledge about the past, but rather how such knowledge is, and should be, communicated to and utilised for the benefit of the public and local communities. Current discussions in archaeologies of engagement are dominated by issues on the role archaeology should play in contemporary society, including matters of social justice, as well as poverty alleviation and economic, social and political empowerment.

A number of issues remain unresolved in the relationship between archaeology and indigenous or aboriginal communities. Sharing the past means allowing alternative interpretations of the archaeological record (Watkins 2005, 442). Indigenous peoples and archaeologists have much to learn from each other, and open communication will help ensure that active learning takes place. Lyn Meskell (2007), in a study of how the past is produced in South Africa, sees the need for:

> ...a radical revisioning of archaeology and anthropology... [*where*]... archaeology labour[*s*] in the service of a newly emergent and more equitable nation, to perform a remedial therapeutic service that actively counteracts the centuries of colonial oppression and apartheid erasures that have deeply affected the production of the past and thus future possibilities. Given this particular historical conjecture, archaeology (like all historical disciplines) is being called upon to do double work, a dual project that seeks to address and redress the past and, through the accounts provided, make possible new understandings of identity in present and future social settings (p. 384).

Southern Africa's complex pasts can only be successfully disentangled when they are shared appropriately among experts and non-experts.

We should concede that heritage is an interesting and important contemporary phenomenon worthy of investigation. The term 'cultural heritage' is really no more than a convenient shorthand, with different contexts of use and different phenomena (material, ideational) it comprises in different parts of the world and for different groups of people. Also, because it is a contemporary phenomenon, any attempt to delineate it also has a tendency to alter it as efforts are made to include a particular heritage (national, regional, ethnic, whatever) within the definition. And that will entail a further redefinition, and so on ad infinitum.

References

Alcock, J. P. H. 1988. Veld types of South Africa. *Memoirs of the Botanical Society of South Africa* 57: 43–44.

Anheier, H. C., and R. Isar, eds. 2011. *Cultures and globalisation: Heritage, memory and identity*. London: Sage Publications.

Aplin, G. 2002. *Heritage identification, conservation and management*. Oxford: Melbourne.

Ashmore, W. and R. J. Sharer. 2009. *Discovering our past: A brief introduction to archaeology*. Mountain View, CA: Mayfield Publishing Company.

Atalay, S. L. 2006. Indigenous archaeology as decolonizing practice. *The American Indian Quarterly* 30 (3 and 4): 280–310.

———. 2007. Global application of indigenous archaeology: Community based participatory research in Turkey. *Archaeologies: Journal of the World Archaeological Congress* 3 (3): 249–270.Babbie, E. R. 1998. *The practice of social research* (8th edition). New York and Belmont, CA: Wadsworth.

Beach, D. N. 1980. *The Shona and Zimbabwe, 900–1850: An outline of Shona history*. Gweru: Mambo Press.

———. 1994. *The Shona and their neighbours*. Oxford: Blackwell.

Bennett, B. 1992. Plants and people of the Amazonian rainforests: The role of ethnobotany in sustainable development. *BioScience* 42: 599–607.

Bent, T. J. 1969 (reprint 1893). *The ruined cities of Mashonaland*. Bulawayo: Books of Rhodesia.

Bhila, H. H. K. 1982. *Trade and politics in a Shona Kingdom: The Manyika and their Portuguese and African neighbours, 1575–1902*. Harare: Longmans. Bicker, A., P. Sillitoe, and J. Pottier, (eds). 2004. *Investigating local knowledge: New directions, new approaches*. Aldershot: Ashgate.

Bless, C. and C. Higson-Smith. 2000. *Fundamentals of social research methods —An African perspective* (3rd edition). Cape Town: Juta and Company Ltd.

Blume, C. L. 2006. Working together developing partnerships with American Indians in New Jersey and Delaware. In *Cross-cultural collaboration: Native peoples and archaeology in the northeastern United States*, edited by J. E. Kerber, 197–212. Lincoln and London, Nebraska: University of Nebraska Press.

Bonner, P., and E. J. Carruthers. 2003. The recent history of the Mapungubwe area. Mapungubwe Cultural Heritage Resources Survey. Unpublished report commissioned by the Department of Environmental Affairs and Tourism.

Boonzaier, E., and A. D. Spiegel. 2008. Tradition. In *New South African keywords,* edited by N. Shephered and S. Robins, 195–208. Johannesburg: Jacana Media; Athens: Ohio University Press.

Borofsky, R.1987. *Making history: Pukapukan and anthropological construction of knowledge.* Cambridge: Cambridge University Press.

Bourdillon, M. 1987. *The Shona peoples: An ethnography of the contemporary Shona, with special references to their religion.* Gweru: Mambo Press.

Bruchac, M., S. Hart, and H. M. Wobst, eds. 2010. *Indigenous archaeologies: A reader on decolonization.* Walnut Creek, California: Left Coast Press.

Bullock, C. 1927. *The Mashona: The indigenous natives of Southern Rhodesia.* Cape Town and Johannesburg: Juta & Company Ltd.

————. 1950. *The Mashona and Matebele.* Cape Town and Johannesburg: Juta and Co. Ltd.

Cahill, Caitlin. 2007. The personal is political: Developing new subjectivities in a participatory action research process. *Gender, Place and Culture* 14 (3): 267–92.

Cahill, Caitlin, and Maria Torre. 2007. Beyond the journal article: Representations, audience, and the presentation of participatory research. In *Connecting people, participation and place: Participatory action research approaches and methods,* edited by S. Kindon, R. Pain and M. Kesby, 196–205. London: Routledge.

Calabrese, J. 2005. Ethnicity, class and polity: The emergence of social and political complexity in the Shashe-Limpopo Valley of southern Africa, AD 900 to 1300. Unpublished PhD thesis, University of the Witwatersrand, Johannesburg.

Carruthers, J. 1992. The Dongola Wild Life Sanctuary: 'Psychological blunder, economic folly and political monstrosity' or 'more value than gold'. *Kleio* 24 (1): 82–100.

————. 2006. Mapungubwe: An historical and contemporary analysis of a World Heritage cultural landscape. *Koedoe* 49 (1): 1–13.

Chapman, R., and K. Randsborg. 1981. Approaches to the archaeology of death. In *The archaeology of death,* edited by R. Chapman, I. Kinnes and K. Randsborg, 1–24. Cambridge: Cambridge University Press.

Chatterton, P., D. Fuller, and P. Routledge. 2007. Relating action to activism: Theoretical and methodological reflections. In Participatory Action Research Approaches and Methods: connecting people, participation and place, edited by Kindon, S., R. Pain and M. Kesby. Routledge Studies in Human Geography, 22. London: Routledge.

Chirikure, S., and G. Pwiti. 2008 Community participation in Archaeology and Heritage Management: Case studies from southern Africa and elsewhere. *Current Anthropology* 49: 467–85.

Chirikure, S., M. Manyanga, W. Ndoro, and G. Pwiti. 2010. Unfulfilled promises? Heritage management and community participation at some of

Africa's cultural heritage sites. *International Journal of Heritage Studies* 16 (1–2): 29–42.

Cisse, L. 2005. The annual festival of the Bulo of Arou: The role of ceremonies, rituals and religious traditons in the conservation and enhancement of Dogon cultural heritage. In *Traditional Conservation Practices in Africa,* edited by Joffroy, T. 89–95. ICCROM Conservation Studies 2. Rome: ICCROM in partnership with African Cultural Heritage Organisations, UNESCO, World Heritage and CRATerre-EAG.

Colcutt, S. 1999. The settings of cultural heritage features. *Journal of Planning Law,* 498–513.

Colwell-Chanthaphonh, C., and T. J. Fergson. 2006. Rethinking abandonment in archaeological contexts. *The SAA Archaeological Record,* 37–41.

Community Ecological Governance. *CEG-News,* No.6 February 2007 (http://www.earthjurisprudence.org/pdf/CEGnewsletter6.pdf) (accessed 2 December 2009).

Cornwall, A., and R. Jewkes. 1995. What is participatory research? *Social Science & Medicine* 41(12): 1667–1676.

Creswell, J. W. 2003. *Research design: Qualitative, quantitative and mixed method approaches.* Thousand Oaks, CA: Sage Publications.

Cunliffe, B., C. Gosden, and R. A. Joyce, eds. 2009. Introduction to *The Oxford Handbook of Archaeology.* Oxford: Oxford University Press.

Cunningham, A. 1996. Professional ethics and ethnobotanical research. In *Selected guidelines for ethnobotanical research,* edited by M. Alexiades and J. Sheldon, 19–51. New York: New York Botanical Garden.

———. 2001. *Applied ethnobotany.* London: Earthscan.

De Maret, P. 1982. The Iron Age in the west and south. In *The archaeology of Central Africa,* edited by Van Noten, F. 77–96. Graz, Austria: Akademische Druck- und Verlagsanstalt.

Dean, R. L., and D. Perrelli. J. 2006. Highway archaeology in Western New York: Archaeologists' views of cooperation between State and Tribal Review Agencies. In *Cross-cultural collaboration: Native peoples and archaeology in the Northeastern United States,* edited by Kerber, J. E., 131–149. Lincoln and London, Nebraska: University of Nebraska Press.

Denzin, N. K. and Y. S. Lincoln, eds. 2011. *Handbook of qualitative research* (4th edition). Thousand Oaks, CA: Sage Publications.

Earle, A., J. Goldin, R. Machiridza, D. Malzbender, E. Manzungu, and T. Mpho. 2006. *Indigenous and institutional profile: Limpopo river basin.* IWMI Working Paper No. 112. Colombo, Sri Lanka: International Water Management Institute.

Edwards, W. 1928. Sacred places. *Native Association Departmental Annual (NADA)* 6: 23–27.

Eloff, J. F. 1979. *Die Kulture van Grefswald: N argeologiese studie van die Ystertdperkkulture op die Plaas Greefswald, Dele I-V.* Pretoria: Universiteit van Pretoria Dept Argeologie.

Evans, C. 1985. Tradition and the cultural landscape: An archaeology of place. *Archaeological Review from Cambridge* 4 (1): 80–94.

Fagan, B. M., D. W. Phillipson and S. G. Daniels. 1969. *Iron Age cultures in Zambia: Dambwa, Ingombe Ilede and the Tonga.* London: Chatto and Windus.

Faulkner, N. 2000. Archaeology from below. *Public Archaeology* 1(1): 21–33.

Fforde, C. 2004. *Collecting the dead: Archaeology and the reburial issue.* London: Duckworth.

Fontein, J. 2006. *The silence of Great Zimbabwe: Contested landscapes and the power of heritage.* London: UCL Press.

Fouche, L., ed. 1937. *Mapungubwe: Ancient Bantu civilisation on the Limpopo.* Pretoria: Government Printer.

Fowler, P. 2003. *World heritage cultural landscapes, 1992–2002.* World Heritage Papers 6. Paris: UNESCO World Heritage Centre.

———. 2004. *Landscapes for the World: Conserving a global heritage.* Macclesfield (UK): Windgather Press.

Friedman, J. 1992. The Past in the Future: History and the politics of identity. *American Anthropologist* 94(4): 837–859.

Gadsby, D. A., S. Colley, B. J. Little, P. A. Shackel, and L. Smith. 2008. Theme 12: Engaged and useful archaeologies. Sixth World Archaeological Congress, Dublin, Ireland, 29 June–4 July 2008, Academic Programme Abstracts, 158–171 (see also www.ucd.ie/wac-6; www.worldarchaeologicalcongress.org)

Gardner, G. J. 1955. Mapungubwe 1935–1940. *South African Archaeological Bulletin* 10: 73–77.

———. 1958. Mapungubwe and the second volume. *South African Archaeological Bulletin* 13: 123–132.

———. 1963. *Mapungubwe Vol. II.* Pretoria: Van Schaik.

Gelfand, M. 1962. *Shona religion (with special reference to the Makorekore).* Cape Town, Wynberg and Johannesburg: Juta & Company Ltd.

Githitho, A. N. 2005. The sacred Mijikenda Kaya forests of coastal Kenya: Traditional conservation and management practices. In *Traditional conservation practices in Africa,* edited by Joffroy, T. 61–67. ICCROM Conservation Studies 2. Rome: ICCROM in partnership with African

Cultural Heritage Organisations, UNESCO, World Heritage and CRATerre-EAG.

Gonçalves, A., and J. Deacon (with contributions from K. Buckley, M. Truscott, and I. Pikirayi). 2004. General report of the scientific symposium on "Place Memory–Meaning: Preserving intangible values in monuments and sites". Fourteenth General Assembly of ICOMOS, Victoria Falls, Zimbabwe, 28–31 October 2003 (http://www.international.icomos.org/victoriafalls2003/finalreport-rapporteurs.pdf).

Greenwood, D. J., W. F. Whyte, and I. Harkavy. 1993. Participatory action research as a process and as a goal. *Human Relations* 46 (2): 175.

Greer, S., R. Harrison, and S. McIntyre-Tamwoy. 2002. Community-based archaeology in Australia. *World Archaeology* 34 (2): 265–287.

Guillaume, M. 1980. *La politique du patrimoine*. Paris: Galilée.

Halbwachs, M. 1980. *The collective memory*. New York: Harper and Row Colophon Books.

————. 1992. The legendary topography of the Gospels in the Holy Land: Conclusion. In *On collective memory*, M. Halbwachs; edited, translated, and introduced by Coser, L. A. 191–235. Chicago and London: University of Chicago Press.

————. 1992. *On collective memory*. Chicago: University of Chicago Press.

Hall, M. 1984. The burden of tribalism: The social context of southern African Iron Age Studies. *American Antiquity* 49 (3), 455–4672.

Hall, S., and B. Smith. 2000. Empowering places: Rock shelters and ritual control in farmer-forager interactions in the Northern Province. In *Africa Naissance: The Limpopo Valley 1000 years ago,* edited by Leslie, M. and T. Maggs, 30–46. The South African Archaeological Society Goodwin Series 8.

Hamilakis, Y., and A. Anagnostopoulos. 2009. What is archaeological ethnography? *Public Archaeology: Archaeological Ethnographies* 8 (2–3): 65–87.

Hanisch, E. 2008. Reinterpreting the origins of Dzata: Archaeology and legends, In *Five hundred years rediscovered: Southern African precedents and prospects,* edited by Swanepoel, N., A. Esterhuysen, and P. Bonner, 119–132. 500 Year Initiative Conference Proceedings, 2007. Johannesburg: Witwatersrand University Press.

Henige, D. P. 1974. *The chronology of oral tradition: Quest for a chimera*. Oxford: Clarendon Press.

————. 1982. *Oral historiography*. New York: Longman.

Hobsbawm, E. 1983. Introduction: Inventing tradition. In *The invention of tradition*, edited by Hobsbawm, E. and T. O. Ranger, 1–14. Cambridge: Cambridge University Press.

Hobsbawm, E., and T. Ranger, eds. 1983. *The invention of tradition*. Cambridge: Cambridge University Press.

Hofmeyer, I. 1989. Turning region into narrative: English storytelling in the Waterberg. In *Holding their ground: Class locality and culture in 19th and 20th century South Africa*, edited by Bonner, P., I. Hofmeyer, D. James, and T. Lodge.

Holleman, J. F. 1952. *Shona customary law with reference to kinship, marriage, the family and the estate*. London: Geofrey Cumberlege: Oxford University Press.

————. 1953. *Accommodating the spirit amongst some north-eastern Shona tribes*. Rhodes-Livingstone Institute Paper 22. Cape Town: Oxford University Press.

————. 1961. Some 'Shona' tribes of Southern Rhodesia. In *Seven tribes of Central Africa*, edited by Colson, E. and M. Gluckman, 354–395. The Institute for Social Research, University of Zambia, and Manchester University.

Holtorf, C. J. 1996. Towards a chronology of Megaliths: Understanding monumental time and cultural memory. *Journal of European Archaeology* 4, 199–152.

Holtorf, C. 2005. *From Stonehenge to Las Vegas: Archaeology as popular culture*. Lanham, MD: AltaMira Press.

————. 2007. *Archaeology is a brand! The meaning of archaeology in contemporary popular culture*. Oxford: Archaeopress.

Horsthemke, K., and J. F. Green. 2008. Indigenous knowledge. *New South African keywords*, edited by Shephered, N. and S. Robins, 128–132. Johannesburg: Jacana Media; Athens: Ohio University Press.

Hubert, J., and C. Fforde. 2002. The reburial issue in the 21st century. In *The dead and their possessions: Repatriation, policy and practice*, edited by Fforde, C., J. Hubert and P. Turnball, 1–16. London: Routledge.

Huffman, T. N. 1996. *Snakes and crocodiles: Power and symbolism in ancient Zimbabwe*. Johannesburg: Witwatersrand University Press.

————. 2000. Mapungubwe and the origins of the Zimbabwe culture. In *Africa Naissance: The Limpopo Valley 1000 years ago*, edited by Leslie, M. and T. Maggs, 14–29). The South African Archaeological Society Goodwin Series 8.

————. 2005. *Mapungubwe: Ancient African civilisation on the Limpopo*. Johannesburg: Witwatersrand University Press.

————. 2007. *Handbook to the Iron Age: The archaeology of pre-colonial farming societies in southern Africa.* Scottsville: University of KwaZulu-Natal Press.

Huffman, T. N., and E. O. M Hanisch. 1987. Settlement hierarchies in the Northern Transvaal: Zimbabwe ruins and Venda history. *African Studies* 46 (1): 79–116.

Hughes, D. O., and T. R. Trautmann, eds. 1995. *Time, histories and ethnologies.* Ann Arbor: University of Michigan Press.

Humphreys, S. C., and H. King. 1981. *Mortality and immortality: The anthropology and archaeology of death.* Proceedings of a meeting of the Research Seminar in Archaeology and Related Subjects held at the Institute of Archaeology, University of London, June 1980. New York and San Diego: Academic Press.

Joffroy, T. 2005, ed. *Traditional conservation practices in Africa.* ICCROM (International Centre for the Study of the Preservation and Restoration of Cultural Property) Conservation Studies 2. Rome: ICCROM and Africa 2009.

Kammen, M. 1991. *Mystic chords of memory: Transformation of tradition in American culture.* New York: Vintage Books.

Kankpeyeng, K. W. 2005. The cultural landscape of Tongo-Tenzuk: Traditional conservation practices. In *Traditional conservation practices in Africa,* edited by T. Joffroy, 15–21. ICCROM Conservation Studies 2. Rome: ICCROM, in partnership with African Cultural Heritage Organisations, UNESCO, World Heritage and CRATerre-EAG.

Kerber, J. E. 2006. Introduction. In *Cross-cultural collaboration: Native peoples and archaeology in the Northeastern United States,* edited by Kerber, J. E., ixx–xxxi. Lincoln and London, Nebraska: University of Nebraska Press.

King, T. F. 2002. *Thinking about cultural resources management: Essays from the edge.* Walnut Creek, CA: AltaMira Press.

————. 2003. *Places that count: Traditional cultural properties in cultural resources management.* Walnut Creek, CA: AltaMira Press.

————. 2008a. *Cultural resource laws and practice.* California, Walnut Creek: AltaMira Press.

————. 2008b. Who makes it heritage. *Heritage Management* 1 (1): 99–107.

Kirshenblatt-Gimblett, B. 2004. Intangible heritage as metacultural production. *Museum International* 56 (1-2): 52-65. Oxford: Blackwell. (http://unesdoc.unesco.org/images/0013/001358/135852e.pdf#135853).

Kretzmann J. P. and J. L. McKnight. 1993. *Building communities from the inside out: A path toward finding and mobilizing a community's assets.* Chicago (IL): ACTA Publications.

Kuper, H., A. J. B. Hughes, and J. van Veslen. 1954. The Shona and Ndebele of Southern Rhodesia. In *Ethnographic Survey of Africa,* edited by Forde, D. Part IV: Southern Africa. London: International African Institute.

Landry, C. 2006. *Culture at the heat of transformation: The role of culture in social and economic development—Lessons learnt from the Swiss Cultural Programme.* Commissioned by the Swiss Agency for Development and Cooperation (SDC) and the Arts Council of Switzerland Pro Helvetia. Bern, Switzerland.

Layton, R. 2001. *Uluru: An aboriginal history of Ayers Rock.* Canberra: Aboriginal Studies Press.

Legassic, M., and C. Rasool. 2000. *Skeletons in the cupboard: South African museums and the trade in human remains, 1907–1917.* Cape Town: South African Museum.

Letellier, R. (with contributions from Werner Schmid and François LeBlanc). 2007. *Recording, documentation and information management for the conservation of heritage places: Guiding principles.* Los Angeles: The Getty Conservation Institute.

Liddle, P. 1985. *Community archaeology: A fieldworker's handbook of organisation and techniques.* Publication 61. Leicester: Leicestershire Museums.

Little, B. J. 2009. What can archaeology do for justice, peace, community, and the Earth? *Historical Archaeology* 43 (4): 115–119.

Loubser, J. H. N. 1988. Archaeological contributions to Venda ethnohistory. PhD thesis, University of the Witwatersrand, Johannesburg.

————. 1992. *The ethnoarchaeology of Venda speakers in Southern Africa.* Novorsinge van die Nasionale Museum Bloemfontein 7, Part 8. Bloemfontein: National Museum.

Lowenthal, D. 1985. *The past is a foreign country.* Cambridge: Cambridge University Press.

————. 2005. Natural and cultural heritage. *International Journal of Heritage Studies* 11 (1): 81–92.

Mafune, I. A. 2010. "An Encounter": A personal encounter of being-becoming an indigenous archaeologist in South Africa. In *Being and becoming indigenous archaeologists,* edited by Nicholas, G. P. 191–198. Walnut Creek, California: Left Coast Press.

Mairi, B. 2005. The protection of the settings of archaeological sites in Scotland. In *Proceedings of the ICOMOS 15th General Assembly and Scientific Symposium,* Vol 1: 27–33. Xian: World Publishing Corporation.

Manyanga, M. 2007. *Resilient landscapes: Socio-environmental dynamics in the Shashi-Limpopo Basin, Southern Zimbabwe, c. AD 800 to the present.*

Studies in Global Archaeology 11. Uppsala: Uppsala University, Uppsala, African and Comparative Archaeology, Department of Archaeology and Ancient History.

Mapunda, B., and P. Lane. 2004. Archaeology for whose interest– archaeologists or the locals? In *Public Archaeology*, edited by Merriman, N. London: Routledge, 211–223.

Maradze, J, 2004. Back to the old school? Revival of traditional management systems in Zimbabwe. Fourteenth General Assembly of ICOMOS and Scientific Symposium, Place – Memory – Meaning: Preserving intangible values in monuments and sites, Victoria Falls, Zimbabwe, 28–31 October 2003.

Marshall, Y. 2002. What is community archaeology? *World Archaeology* 34 (2): 211–219.

―――. 2009. Community archaeology. In *The Oxford handbook of archaeology*, edited by Cunliffe, B., C. Gosden and R. A. Joyce, 1078–1102. Oxford: Oxford University Press.

Marufu, A. 2008. A comparative study of the material culture from settlement and mortuary contexts in northern Zimbabwe—the case of Musengezi tradition. MA dissertation, University of Dar es Salaam.

Mason, R. 1962. *Prehistory of the Transvaal: A record of human activity.* Johannesburg: Witwatersrand University Press.

―――. 1973. The Limpopo Mobile Belt, South Africa. *Philosophical transactions of the Royal Society of London.* Series A. Mathematical and Physical Sciences 273 (1235): 463–485.Matowanyika, J. Z. Z. 2000. *Indigenous knowledge systems in environmental education within communities in Southern Africa.* Howick, South Africa: SADC Regional Environmental Education Centre (REEC), Umgeni Valley Project.

McClanahan, A. 2007. The cult of community: Defining the 'local' in public archaeology and heritage discourse. In *Which past, whose future? The past at the start of the 21st century*, edited by Grabow, S., D. Hull and E. Waterton 51–57. Oxford: Archaeopress.

McDonald, E. M., B. Coldrick, and L. Villiers. 2005. *Study of aboriginal cultural values associated with groundwater-related environmental features on the Gnangara Mound.* Report prepared by Estill & Associates Pty Ltd for the Department of Environment. Available for download @: http://portal.water.wa.gov.au/portal/page/portal/WaterManagement/Ground w.

McIntyre, A. 2008. *Participatory action research.* Los Angeles: Sage Publications.

Merriman, N., ed. 2004. *Public archaeology*. London: Routledge.

Meskell, L. 2007. Falling wall and mending fences: Archaeological ethnography in the Limpopo. *Journal of Social Archaeology* 33 (2): 383–400.

Meyer, A. 1998. *The archaeological sites of Greefswald*. Pretoria: University of Pretoria Press.

Mgijima, B., and V. Buthelezi. 2006. Mapping museum-community relations in Lawndale. *Journal of Southern African Studies* 32 (4): 795–806.

Mitchell, P. 2002. *The archaeology of Southern Africa*. Cambridge: Cambridge University Press.

Mothulatshipi, S. M. 2009. Landscape archaeology of the later farming communities of the Shashe-Limpopo Basin, eastern Botswana: Landuse diversity and human behaviour. Unpublished PhD thesis, University of Edinburgh.

Msemwa, P. 2005. Community perception of heritage resources: Conflicting interests. In *Salvaging Tanzania's cultural heritage*, edited by Mapunda, B. B. B. and P. Msemwa, 236–242. Dar es Salaam: Dar es Salaam University Press.

Munjeri, D. 2004. Tangible and intangible heritage: From difference to convergence. *Museum International* 56 (1–2); 12–19 (http://unesdoc.unesco.org/images/0013/001358/135852e.pdf#135853).

Ndlovu, N. 2010. Archaeological battles and triumphs: A personal reflection. In *Being and becoming indigenous archaeologists,* edited by Nicholas, G. P., 222–234. Walnut Creek, California: Left Coast Press.

Ndoro, W. 2001. *Your monument our shrine: The preservation of Great Zimbabwe*. Studies in African Archaeology 19. Uppsala: Societas Archaeologica Upsaliensis.

———. 2004. Traditional and customary heritage systems, nostalgia or reality? The implications of managing heritage sites in Africa. In *Linking universal and local values: Managing a sustainable future for world heritage,* edited by de Merode, E., R. Smeets and C. Westrik, 81–84. Paris: UNESCO.

———. 2005. *The preservation of Great Zimbabwe: Your monument our shrine.* ICCROM Conservation Studies 4. Rome: ICCROM.

———. 2008. Legal definitions of Heritage. In *Cultural heritage and the law: Protecting immovable heritage in English-speaking countries of sub-Saharan Africa.* ICCROM Conservation Studies 8. Rome: ICCROM in partnership with African cultural heritage organizations, UNESCO World Heritage Centre, CRATerre, ENSAG, CHDA, and EPA.

Ndoro, W., and G. Pwiti. 2001. Heritage management in southern Africa: Local, national and international discourse. *Public Archaeology* 2: 21–34.

Ndoro, W., and G. Pwiti. 2005. *Legal frameworks for the protection of immovable cultural heritage in Africa.* ICCROM Conservation Studies 5.

Africa 2009 Conservation of Immovable Cultural Heritage in Sub-Saharan Africa. Rome: ICCROM in partnership with African cultural heritage organizations, UNESCO World Heritage Centre and CRATerre-EAG.

Ndoro, W., and S. Chirikure. 2009. Debates in African heritage management. *Heritage International.*

Ndoro, N., A. Mumma, and G. Abungu. 2008. *Cultural heritage and the law: Protecting immovable heritage in English-speaking countries of sub-Saharan Africa.* ICCROM Conservation Studies 8. Rome: ICCROM in partnership with African cultural heritage organizations, UNESCO World Heritage Centre, CRATerre, ENSAG, CHDA and EPA.

Nienaber, W. C. 2007. Report on the archaeological investigation of localities indicated as the possible burial place of Chief Fadana and his companions, Robben Island. Archive file at the Dept of Anatomy, University of Pretoria.

Nienaber, W. C., M. Steyn, and L. Hutten. 2008. The grave of King Mgolombane Sandile Ngqika: Revisiting the legend. *South African Archaeological Bulletin* 63 (187): 46–50.

Nienaber, C., N. Keough, M. Steyn, and J. H. Meiring. 2008. Reburial of the Mapungubwe human remains: An overview of the process and procedure. *South African Archaeological Bulletin* 63 (188): 164–169.

Nienaber, W. C., and M. Steyn. 2002. Archaeology in the service of the community: The repatriation of the remains of Nontetha Bungu. *South African Archaeological Bulletin* 57 (176): 80–84.

Nienaber, W.C., and M. Hutten. 2006. *The 2003 Mapungubwe Stabilization Project.* Conducted as Phase II of the Mapungubwe Cultural Landscape Rehabilitation Project. Business Enterprises at the University of Pretoria Pty (Ltd), for South African Heritage Resources Agency (SAHRA).Nachmias, D. and C. Nachmias. 1981. *Research methods in the social sciences.* New York: St Martin's Press.

Odora Hoppers, C.A., ed. 2002. *Indigenous knowledge and the integration of knowledge systems.* Claremont, Cape Town: New Africa Books.

Onjala, I. O., and E. K. Kamaru. 2005. Thimlich Ohinga: Traditional conservation practices. In *Traditional conservation practices in Africa,* edited by Joffroy, T. 97–104. ICCROM (International Centre for the Study of the Preservation and Restoration of Cultural Property) Conservation Studies 2. Rome: ICCROM.

Pearson, P. M. 2003. *The Archaeology of death and burial.* Sutton: Stroud.

Peel, J. D.Y. 1984. Making history: The past in the Ijesha present. *Man* 19: 111–132.

Petzet, M. 2004. Principles of preservation: An introduction to the International Charters for Conservation and Restoration, 40 years after the Venice Charter. *Monuments and Sites* 1. Paris: ICOMOS.

Pikirayi, I. 1987. Musengezi: The description and characterisation of a later Iron Age sub-tradition in northern Zimbabwe. MA thesis, University of Zimbabwe.

————. 1993. *The Archaeological identity of the Mutapa State: Towards an historical archaeology of northern Zimbabwe.* Studies in African Archaeology 6. Uppsala: Societas Archaeologica Upsaliensis.

————. 2001. *The Zimbabwe culture: Origins and decline in southern Zambezian states.* Walnut Creek, California: AltaMira Press.

————. 2006. The Kingdom, the power and forevermore: Zimbabwe culture in contemporary art and architecture. *Journal of Southern African Studies* 32 (4): 755–770.

————. 2007. Public involvement in Archaeological excavations in southern Africa. In *From concepts of the past to practical strategies: The teaching of archaeological field techniques,* P. Ucko, Q. Ling and J. Hubert, 305–320. London: Saffron Books.

Pikirayi, I. 2009. What can archaeology do for society in southern Africa? *Historical Archaeology* 43(4), 125–127.

Pikirayi, I. 2011. The past within the present: The contemporary uses of Mapungubwe. In Tiley-Nel, S. (ed), *Mapungubwe remembered: Contributions to Mapungubwe by the University of Pretoria.* Johannesburg: Chris van Rensburg Publications, 262–271.

Posselt, F. W. T. 1927. *A survey of the native tribes of southern Rhodesia.* Salisbury: Government of Southern Rhodesia.

————. 1930. Ethnographic sketch of the natives of Southern Rhodesia. *Official Yearbook of Southern Rhodesia* 2: 750–61. Salisbury: Government Printer.

————. 1935. *Fact and fiction: A short account of the natives of Southern Rhodesia.* Bulawayo: Rhodesian Printing and Publishing Co.

Pwiti, G. 1996a. Let the ancestors rest in peace? New challenges for heritage management in Zimbabwe. *Conservation and Management of Archaeological Sites* 1(3): 151–160.

————. 1996b. Peasants, chiefs and kings: A model of the development of cultural complexity in northern Zimbabwe. *Zambezia* 23 (1): 31–52.

Pwiti, G., and G. Mahachi. 1991. Shona ethnography and the interpretation of Iron Age burials: The significance of burial location. *Zimbabwea* 1: 57–9.

Pyburn, A. 2003. Archaeology for a New Millennium: The rules of engagement. In *Archaeologists and local communities,* edited by Derry, L. and M. Malloy, 167–184. Washington, D.C.: Society for American Archaeology.

————. 2007. Archeology as activism. In *Cultural heritage and human rights,* edited by Silverman, H. and D. F. Ruggles, 172–180. New York: Springer.

————. 2009. Practicing Archaeology – as if it really matters. *Public Archaeology: Archaeological Ethnographies* 8 (2–3): 161–175.

Rakatomamonjy, B., and A. Napon. 2005. The Na-Yiri of Kokologho. In *Traditional conservation practices in Africa*, edited by Joffroy, T. 7–11. ICCROM Conservation Studies 2. Rome: ICCROM in partnership with African Cultural Heritage Organisations, UNESCO, World Heritage and CRATerre-EAG.

Ralushai, N. M. N., and J. R. Gray. 1977. Ruins and traditions of the Ngona and the Mbedzi among the Venda of the northern Transvaal. *Rhodesian History* 8: 1–11.

Ralushai, V. N. 2005. Oral history of Mapungubwe. Unpublished Report.

Raphael, T., and D. Quan. 2002. International course on preventive conservation strategies for collections in Southeast Asia (CollAsia 2010). Thailand: Sponsored by ICCROM and SPAFA.

Redford, K., and J. Mansour, eds. 1998. *Traditional peoples and biodiversity conservation in large tropical landscapes*. Rosslyn (VA): The Nature Conservancy.

Redford, K., and C. Padoch, eds. 1992. *Conservation of neotropical forests: Working from traditional resource use*. New York: Columbia University Press.

Renzetti, C. M. and R. M. Lee, (eds). 1993. *Researching sensitive topics*. Sage Publications.

Reser, J. P. and J. M. Bentrupperbäumer. 2005. What and where are environmental values? Assessing the impacts of current diversity of use of 'environmental' and 'World Heritage' values. *Journal of Environmental Psychology* 25 (2), 125–146.

Richards, J. B. 1942. Mlimo: Beliefs and practices of the Karanga. *Native Association Departmental Annual (NADA)* 19.Riegl, A. 1996. *The modern cult of monuments: Its character and its origin*. In Price, N. S., M. K., Tall (Jr.) and A. M. Vaccaro, (eds), *Historical and philosophical issues in the conservation of cultural heritage*. Los Angeles: Getty Conservation Institute.

Riley, M. and D. Harvey. 2005. Landscape archaeology, heritage and community in Devon: An oral history approach. *International Journal of Heritage Studies*, 11 (4), 269–288.

Roskies, D. G. 1999. *The Jewish search for a usable past: The Helen and Martin Schwartz lectures in Jewish studies*. Bloomington: Indiana University Press.

Sauer, E. 2004. *Archaeology and ancient history: Breaking down the boundaries*. London and New York: Routledge.

Schipper, F. T., and M. T. Bernhardsson. 2010. Archaeology in conflict: Setting the agenda. *Forum Archaeologiae* 55 (6) (http://farch.net).

Schoeman, M. H. 2006. Imagining rain places: Rain control and changing ritual landscapes in the Shashe-Limpopo confluence area, South Africa. *South African Archaeological Bulletin* 61 (184): 152–165.Schoeman, M. H. and I. Pikirayi. 2011. Repatriating more than Mapungubwe human remains: Archaeological material culture, a shared future and an artificially divided past. *Journal of Contemporary African Studies* 29 (4), 389–403.

Selier, J. 2007. Counting elephants in the Tuli. *Mashatu Trunk Call*, Newsletter August 2007 edition (http://www.mashatu.com), 2–5.Setlhabi, K. G. 2010. *Documentation of material culture: A study of the ethnology division of Botswana National Museum.* PhD thesis, University of Botswana.

Shackel, P. A. 2007. Civic engagement and social justice: Race on the Illinois frontier. In *Archaeology as a tool of civic engagement,* Little, B. J. and P. A. Shackel, 243–262. Lanham, MD: AltaMira Press.

Shepherd, N. 2007. Archaeology dreaming: Post-apartheid urban imaginaries and the bones of the Prestwich Street dead. *Journal of Social Archaeology* 7 (1): 3–28.

————. 2008. Heritage. In *New South African keywords,* edited by N. Shephered and S. Robins, 116–128. Johannesburg: Jacana Media; Athens: Ohio University Press.

Singleton, T. A., and C. E. Orser (Jr.). 2003. Descendant communities: Linking people in the present to the past. In *Ethical issues in archaeology,* edited by L. J. Zimmerman, K. D. Vitelli and J. Hollowell-Zimmer, 143–152. Walnut Creek, California: AltaMira Press.

Smith, J. M. 2005. Climate change and agropastoral sustainability in the Shashe-Limpopo River Basin from AD 900. Unpublished PhD thesis, University of the Witwatersrand, Johannesburg.

Stayt, H. A. 1931. *The BaVenda.* Oxford: Oxford University Press for the International African Institute.

Stewart, R., A. Clark, and M. Fulford. 2004. Promoting inclusion: Facilitating access to the Silchester 'town life' project. *World Archaeology* 34 (2): 220–235.

Steyn, M. 1997. A reassessment of the human skeletons from K2 and Mapungubwe, South Africa. *South African Archaeological Bulletin* 51: 14–20.

————. 1998. A review of the skeletal remains from the Greefswald sites. In *The archaeological sites of Greefswald,* by Meyer, A. 287–291. Pretoria: University of Pretoria Press.

Steyn, M., and M. Henneberg. 1995. Pre-Columbian presence of Treponemal Disease: A possible case from Iron Age southern Africa. *Current Anthropology* 36 (5): 869–873.

————. 1996. Skeletal growth of children from the Iron Age site at K2, South Africa. *American Journal of Physical Anthropology* 100 (3): 389–396.

Steyn, M., and W.C. Nienaber. 2005. Repatriation of human remains in South Africa. In *Voyages in science: Essays by South African anatomists in honour of Philip V. Tobias's 80th birthday*, edited by Strakalj, G., N. Panther and B. Kramer, 159–177. Pretoria: Content Solutions.

Stoecker, R. 1999. Are academics irrelevant? Roles for scholars in participatory research. *American Behavioral Scientist* 42 (5): 840–854.

Sutton, J. E. G. 1994–1995. The growth of farming communities in Africa from the equator southwards. *Azania* 29–30. Nairobi: British Institute in Eastern Africa.

Tolman, D., and M. Brydon-Miller. 2001. Interpretive and participatory research methods: Moving toward subjectivities. In *From subjects to subjectivities: A handbook of interpretive and participatory methods*, edited by Tolman, D. and M. Brydon-Miller, 3–11. New York: New York University Press.

Ucko, P. 1969. Ethnography and archaeological interpretation of funerary remains. *World Archaeology* 1: 262–80.

Van Riet Lowe, C. 1936. Mapungubwe: First report on excavations in the northern Transvaal. *Antiquity* 10 (39): 282–291.

Van Warmelo, N. J. 1932. *Contributions towards Venda history, religion and tribal ritual*. Ethnological Publication 3. Pretoria: Government Printer.

————, ed. 1942. The copper mines of Musina and the early history of the Zoutpansberg. *Ethnological Publications*. Vol. VIII. Pretoria: Government Printer.

————. 1960. *Contributions towards Venda history, religion and tribal ritual*. Union of South Africa, Department of Native Affairs: Government Printers.

Vansina, J. 1985. *Oral tradition as history*. Madison: University of Wisconsin Press.

Voigt, E. A. 1983. *Mapungubwe: An archaeological interpretation of an Iron Age community*. Pretoria: Transvaal Museum Monograph No. 1.

Watkins, J. 2003. Archaeological ethics and American Indians. In *Ethical issues in archaeology*, edited by Zimmerman, L. J., K. D. Vitelli and J. Hollowell-Zimmer, 130–141. Walnut Creek, CA: AltaMira.

————. 2005. Through wary eyes: Indigenous perspectives on archaeology. *Annual Review of Anthropology* 34: 429–49.

————. 2006. Foreword. In *Cross-cultural collaboration: Native peoples and archaeology in the Northeastern United States*, edited by Kerber, J. E., xi–xvi. Lincoln and London, Nebraska: University of Nebraska Press.

Watkins, J., and J. Beaver. 2008. What do we mean by "Heritage"? *Heritage Management* 1 (1): 9–35.

Weinrich, A. K. H. 1971. *Chiefs and councils in Rhodesia: Transition from patriarchal to bureaucratic power.* London: Heinemann.

About the Book

This book captures community voices in matters relating to their relationship with specific archaeological heritage sites and landscapes in the Limpopo Province of South Africa. Focusing on the stonewalled archaeological heritage associated with Venda speakers and the reburial in 2008 of human remains excavated by the University of Pretoria from the cultural landscape of Mapungubwe, the book attempts to establish why archaeology and cultural heritage conservation struggle for relevance in South Africa today.

In articulating the relevance of archaeology in South Africa in particular and southern Africa in general and in the context of public or community-based archaeology, the book explores how communities and the public interact, use and negotiate with their pasts. The research critiques the notion of archaeological heritage conservation and attempts to understand cultural heritage conservation from the perspectives of descendant communities. The book further exposes the conflict between cultural heritage protection efforts and modern development and questions the role of such efforts, given the challenges of unemployment, social inequality and poverty in democratic South Africa. The book is also about community engagement in archaeology, specifically in matters relating to access to cultural heritage resources. This study suggests that there is scope for community archaeology to take centre-stage and drive future directions in archaeology if archaeologists change their approach in dealing with communities.

Researchers are challenged in this study to rethink the notion of heritage, to debate the objectives behind cultural heritage conservation and to critically re-examine the relevance of archaeology today. This study suggests that the conflicting positions between heritage managers, archaeologists and descendant communities may be resolved through sharing of 'tradition' with the 'present'.

About the Author

Innocent Pikirayi is a Professor in Archaeology at the University of Pretoria. He researches the southern African later Iron Age, specifically the archaeology of Mapungubwe, Great Zimbabwe and post Great Zimbabwe periods. His primary interest in cultural heritage focuses on the relationships between archaeology and the public, specifically on the relevance of archaeological practice to descendant communities. He has been involved with the repatriation of human remains to the Mapungubwe Cultural Landscape and World Heritage Site and is working closely with the relevant South African government departments, communities from the Limpopo Province of South Africa and stakeholders to determine how infrastructure development and cultural heritage conservation can best intersect with each other. He can be contacted at innocent.pikirayi@up.ac.za